For a fellow Francophile
Aloha.
Karen
tutu ♡

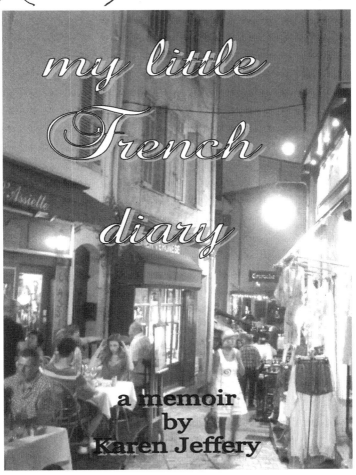

my little

French

diary

a memoir
by
Karen Jeffery

Praise for my little French diary:

La plus belle cote du monde indeed! With stories and pictures to match...My BIG French diary. Patrick Snow, International best-selling author of <u>Creating your own Destiny</u>, <u>The Affluent Entrepreneur</u>, and <u>Boy Entrepreneur</u>

Bonjour. Buongiorno. From the Italian part of France to the French part of Italy, Karen shares the cultural history through photographs and little vignettes like a kiss on both cheeks. David Snow, talk show host. doctorhealthradio.com

Picasso, Monet, Chagall, St. Tropez, Nice, Antibes, Film Festivals and Yachting Festivals ...and Karen Jeffery! Wow!! Amy Ritch, reformed attorney, keynote speaker and coach, author of <u>Reclaiming your Joy</u>.

Monte Carlo to St. Tropez, the Cote d'Azur to the heart of Provence, Cinque Terre to Florence - this memoir sings! (in French). Jasmin Akash, founder Akash Khi Healing Center. Master Healer and Author: <u>Holographic Meditation - the 12 Elixirs of Life</u> and <u>Akash Khi Alphabet</u>

Let Karen take you on the trip of your life. You won't be disappointed. And with any luck, you'll be booking your own sojourn on the dazzling Cote d'Azur. PJ Panzica, International Sailor, Filmmaker, Owner - Lighthouse Productions.

Karen's memoir is a life-filled adventure. Fasten your seatbelt. This is a trip you will want to experience! Lyla Berg, PhD, Author, <u>Leaving the Guilded Cage</u>

A feast for the eyes and the senses, the imagination and the heart. Brought back many memories and a strong desire to tour Europe again.
Fred Spanjaard, GlobalMediaProductions.com

The chapter of the little island, Sanctuary - that stole my heart. Ahhhhhh. Suzan Proia, C. Hr, EPC, author of <u>Finding your Answers Within,</u> Speaker, professional coach, EFT Practitioner,

We have so much to learn from the French...and from Karen, an American journalist who chronicled it all...with some side trips to Italy.
Yoellah Yududah, artist and author, <u>Black Woman's Odyssey in Israel.</u>

Insight and information about this fabulous slice of the world. Something you should not miss -- like this book. Riki Inzano, Artist, Sculptor.

I was hooked at the introduction, and by the time we landed in Villefranche sur Mer I had a French addiction. The language, the culture, the art, the wine - what's not to love?!!
Jayne Bush, <u>Winning at Losing</u>

Whether you love France (yet) or not, you'll want to dive into Karen's world. Edie Van Hoose, <u>Hawaiian Meditations</u>

An American journalist heads off to cover the Côte d'Azur, enjoys French culture and food, lives with wine-making monks on a tiny island. What a sublime adventure! You won't just read this book, you'll experience the French Riviera with Karen as your guide. Nicole Kristin Gabriel, Owner & Manager, Angel Dog Productions, author of <u>Finding Your Inner Truth</u> and <u>Stepping into Your Becoming.</u>

There's no more experienced writer, and Karen offers insight for both the inexperienced and the regular traveler to the South of France. A must read. Sylvia Cabral, teacher.

I had never been outside North America until I read this book. Then I was transported to France, smack into the middle of the Cannes Film Festival. I had a press pass for god's sake. That press pass was a magic ticket. I could go anywhere and talk to everyone. In reality, the author took me on that trip. You won't read this book. Really, you won't. You will experience it... if you let yourself. It's just that damn good.
Stuart O'Neill, Business and Political Consultant.

COPYRIGHTS

Editing, Layout, Design, and Cover Art by

Resource Unlimited
Publisher

Visit website at:
www.mauiwriter.com/resource
First Printing: July, 2015
ISBN-10:0989992535
ISBN-13:978-0-9899925-3-4

This book is also available in all ebook formats.
Visit: www.mauiwriter.com/frenchdiary

Also by the author:
Hot Tickets!! ~ A Week on Maui
Cuba Notes ~ insights on the forbidden island
Neosomaniac ~ Mad about Islands
Coconut Cuisine ~ the secret of happy islanders

Merci Beaucoup

As always ~ big thanks to my family and friends who cheerlead whenever I head out on a new adventure, dropping everything to fly half-way around the world, indulging my wanderlust.

With gratitude and love for my three children, for my birth family, my created family, and my global family.

And to the new friends I make on every journey and come to love like family. To all the beautiful souls I met in France who opened their hearts and showed me different ways of living and caring.

To all the writers I have read and loved and to those who have always encouraged my writing. Fellow writers, editors, poets, artists ~ you inspire me every day, give me the green light to forge on, exploring the unique places of this amazing planet and the interior and exterior journeys.

And special thanks to my readers. You encourage me to keep on traveling...and writing.

Bless you all.

"Sounds of laughter shades of love are ringing through my open ears, inciting and inviting me. Limitless undying love which shines around me like a million suns, it calls me on and on across the universe..." John Lennon

Bonjour mes amis,

This project ~ a memoir of my sojourn along the Côte d'Azur ~ began in my dreams while visiting my son in Thailand in March, 2014. I envisioned it as the ultimate writer's workshop: six months in fabulous France. By May I was in Cannes with my press pass, just in time to cover the Film Festival then settle in for a sweet little adventure.

Immersing myself in the language, studying French at Nice's International House, I enjoyed nearly every museum, gallery, and cultural venue along the Côte d'Azur.

I interviewed film buffs, expats, and yachties, made discoveries and friends, and spent a week with wine-making monks on an angelic island. I shot over 2500 photos and tried to keep up with an ambitious blog, while becoming an 'Explorer' and 'Top Contributor' to Trip Advisor. The adventure lit my creative fires.

There were side trips to Italy - Rome, Florence, and the unforgettable Cinque Terre - and jaunts into Provence, but mostly I lived along the dazzling coastline of the French Riviera. I wish everyone could visit this special part of the globe sometime, to experience its wonders, its charming people, and its enviable lifestyle.

CONTENTS

"Come, come, whoever you are. Wanderer, worshiper, lover of leaving.
 It doesn't matter.
Ours is not a caravan of despair.
Come, even if you have broken your vows a thousand times.
Come, yet again, come, come."

Rumi

13 Mai

Up at the Villa

I finally make it to the Villa Jardins, Ephrussi de Rothschild[3], and words can't describe it, so I'll let the photos do the talking:

Villa Jardins, Ephrussi de Rothschild
http://mauiwriter.com/villa

The palace is filled with historic art collections, built during the Belle Époque by and for Russian royalty, Beatrice Ephrussi de Rothschild. The fantastic gardens wrap around the estate and are separately French, Florentine, Rose, Japanese, Stone, Exotic, Spanish, and Provençal. These

---

[3] http://www.villa-ephrussi.com/en/home

especially were dear to the heart of Beatrice. I decide then and there to come back next life as a baroness.

Instead at five, I take the 81 back to Villefranche, stop in a little shop for a local red wine, brie and baguette, ripe cherries, then walk back downhill to my hotel.

I'm a bit sunburnt, but what a first day in France! Before long, the full moon is rising over the bay on my sweet little paradise.

Good night moon.

14 Mai

Sur la Plage

I'm thinking I need a beach day, since I've had two days of travel marathon. I grab a ham sandwich on a half-baguette at a café by the harbor, then make my way to the beach by mid-morning. The sun is hot. Bronze women swim and lie topless, one with an amazing four-color tattoo on her left breast.

Soon I am hot enough to dare the brisk water and I swim as if to shake off the long flight and a mainland winter. Then sunning, I people-watch and listen to children playing. Parents buy them ice cream. Tourists chat. Lovers kiss. The train sneaks by.

Strolling over to La Dolce Vita, I buy a chilled rosé and watch little boats in the harbor, returning later to my towel. Just to sit. On a picture perfect day. With nothing to do. Nowhere to be. Bliss.

The streets are quiet. No cruise ships come on Wednesdays, so many shops and restaurants are closed. Locals hang out, chatting in doorways. The town is like a small village again. Walking back through the old town, I drop into the Chapelle de Saint Pierre des Pêcheurs, a lovely little Romanesque chapel designed and painted by Jean Cocteau. Creative and colorful frescoes cover the walls and ceiling, filling the structure with both spiritual and symbolic meaning.

I wander the back streets with my camera, then stop for dinner at La Grignotiere, where Brigitte serves me duck breast in fig, julienne of carrot, broccolini and courgette flan, potatoes au gratin, baby tomatoes, and a beautiful glass of red wine.

Françoise Scoftudcer.
Waitress. Cannes.
"Beaucoup du monde et ici. (Many of the world are here.) All these people are good for business, especially after our slow winter. These two weeks of crazy kick off our busy season, so everything's better now until September.

23 Mai

Nice

There are no money changers in the town of Villefranche sur Mer, and I've run out of Euros, requiring a daytrip to Nice. I go by train (€1.70), then take a tram to Massena Square. It's early morning still, so I walk the Promenade, noting how aqua the water is. Immediately I grok the whole Cote d'Azur thing.

Then I catch a hop on-hop off, open air bus, shooting pictures of buildings, people, parks and gardens. Nice smells like roses and jasmine as we swing past the Modern Art Museum with its modern architecture and sculpted reminder to think outside the box. The bus winds its way uphill to a quiet residential area with older houses and buildings from the Belle Epoch[4].

The Chagall Museum houses the largest permanent collection of the artist's work, so when I figure it might take too long, I save it for another day. The Matisse Museum sits in a park,

---

[4] "Beautiful Era". Conventionally dated from 1871 to the outbreak of World War I in 1914. It was characterized by optimism, regional peace, economic prosperity and technological and scientific innovations. In the climate of the period, especially in Paris, the arts flourished. Many masterpieces of literature, music, theater, and visual art gained recognition. The *Belle Époque* was considered a golden age. (Wikipedia)

filled with olive groves, and today is a special holiday for children. It's the Jour des Enfants (Children's Day). The space buzzes with laughter. Inside docents are teaching art appreciation to four-year olds! The children sit quietly - learning, respectful, happy.

I'm beginning to love French public spaces. They're clean and beautiful, down to their bathrooms, and they're not locked like back home or "private, just for employees." Most museums are free. Music and concerts too. In the states we've sold off so much of our common space. It's nice to see culture handled so well and for the benefit of the people.

I reach the Franciscan church and gardens via Miles Davis Avenue, then stop to smell the roses. After registering for my French classes, which start Monday at the International House (www.ihnice.com), I get back on the bus and zoom off to the Port with more stories in my earpiece of the Ruskies arriving, Italians, les petit histoires du Côte (little stories of the coast).

I jump off at the famous Cours Saleya, brimming with flower and produce stalls, cafés, handicraft shops. Café Paradice calls to my growling stomach, and as I settle in with a fresh seafood pasta, another Senegalese comes from the kitchen. They're ubiquitous, like Ecuadorians in New York restaurants, starting as dishwashers, becoming some of the best chefs on the Riviera.

Strolling back along the promenade and through the gardens, I stop at the US consulate, next on my 'to do' list, but the office is closed due to a lack of staff. When I call the number posted in front, I'm told I need to go to Paris. Seriously, they can't find someone to take a job in Nice?!

The train back takes ten minutes, and by six I'm back in Villefranche, after the daily obligatory six to ten miles of walking. I pour a glass of wine and put my feet up. It feels like home.

24 Mai

La Trinquette

I am greeted and seated at a port-side table with sprigs of fresh jasmine and a great view of the band. I begin with a Chateau de la Bonneliere sauvignon blanc, bread and olives. Salade de la Darse showcases the freshest local seafood - poupes, gambas, et hareng (octopus, jumbo prawns, herring). Then flan de legumes maison, another wine.

I study the menu. La Trinquette serves all local products and dishes, cuisine traditional: fish soup, lobster, seafood pasta, steaks. Home made desserts include tarte aux pommes (apple tart), mousse au chocolat, crème brûlée, crème glacée (ice cream). I indulge and order the tart.

Named after the trinquette, the small staysail on a sailboat, the restaurant was established by Joseph Jean-Charles de Marseilles in 1963. It's still a family affair, with Jean Charles Vernay, proprietor and founder's grandson, waiting on me. His eyes twinkle as he tells the stories.

It's modern jazz this weekend, featuring guitar virtuoso, Pierre Bertrand. The band eats first, taking the stage at about eight. The €5 cover for the musicians shows up on the bill. Even in this warm, family bistro, 50-70 diners at €5 each is about €300 for the band, plus tips. Musician friends back home would love this.

A favorite of Paul McCartney, Roger Moore, and other celebrities, La Trinquette is also enjoyed by locals and enjoys a wonderful history. Since the early years La Trinquette has been in the old port of La Darse, supporting oceanic sciences, students, and sailors from the French Navy when they're in port. Its long sailing tradition is not just in its name. It's in its vibe and its atmosphere.

And the jazz rocks.

25 Mai

La Citadelle

Earlier in the day I walk up to the Poste to buy a French telephone. It's not a smart phone, but it's cheap at E15. Despite good wireless in the hotel for emails, skyping, and texting, I can't make phone calls, and I need to. The hotel is booked after tomorrow, and another place is essential. So I'm all over Air BnB.

The annual flower show just finished at the Citadelle, but two free museums and lovely gardens welcome me on my way home. The main show is Volti, a sculptor and French treasure.

Enjoy!
http://www.mauiwriter.com/citadelle

28 Mai

Changes in Altitude

Je pense que six mois à un nouvel endroit peut être un changeur de vie.

I'm thinking that six months somewhere new can be a life changer. Today I wake under a light duvet after a solid sleep. I rearrange the kitchen while plunging coffee. I've moved from Hotel la Darse into a darling little one-bedroom apartment in the old town. I am the first tenant. It's owned by Britts and brand spanking new, with state of the art kitchen, appliances, and more...in a building centuries old.

Last night I discover a button on the tv remote that changes the language. I watch three old episodes of Friends while fixing and enjoying dinner. Did I mention that EVERYTHING here tastes better? The chicken is phenomenal. Eggs are lovely. Veggies - superb. Butter is better. Olive oil is holy.

I walk up the hill to the marché, thinking about marché and marché (walk and the market, both spelled the same). It's the length of the park, and I am enchanted by the sights, smells, people cueing up for...vegetables! First I get maps and info from Crystel at the Tourism Office. France does tourism offices very well. At Odele Cohen's Italian silk fashion booth, I run into Hazel and

Lynn, London gals I met at La Trinquette, on their way to Monte Carlo on the bus. They help me select a breezy taupe silk blouse, something a bit more French than my t-shirt wardrobe.

The square in the morning buzzes with activity. I buy veggies at the market, then enjoy a café at the bar Chez Betty, while watching a Villefranche rush hour. Downhill towards Rue Poilu, I visit le boucher, le Casino (not a casino but a little corner market, perfect for crème fraîche and toilet paper), la patisserie (oui oui).

On the way home, a couple stops me for directions. "Parlez vous English?" they ask, tongues stumbling. I chuckle inside then direct them to the bus stop, suggesting they stop at the market on the way.

I make a little salad with greens, chicken, blue cheese, olives, enjoying it on my balcony with plenty of sun and a chilled sauterne.

I'm learning to nap. Back from a visit to la poste, to change the language on my new little tele to English (so I can dial, store numbers, answer), I curl up and fall into a deep sleep for two hours. And wake delighted. This is a habit I've neither practiced nor perfected, like my father did. It always feels strange when I attempt a nap. Usually I cannot sleep, but often twenty minutes in silence does the trick. Today I sleep.

In the late afternoon I meet a lovely man at the beach. He buys me un café, and we speak French for two hours, walking along the seaside. He's convinced I can be fluent in two months. I must admit I'm getting better. Comprehension is good, speaking is still difficult, although I wake with French childhood songs in my head and speak French on my tele. He's lovely, from Nice, born in Italy. He orders a Marguerite, like the original pizza from Napoli (just down the coast), and we sit at Port Santé, enjoying pizza and watching les poissons, les bateaux, le soleil gradation (the fish, the boats, the sunset).

Sweet days trail each other as I change my eating and exercise patterns, shopping and sleeping habits, language, friends...and wonder who and where I will be at the end of this journey.

A few more neighborhood shots here:
http://www.mauiwriter.com/vsm2

30 Mai

Je Pense que c'est la plus belle cote du monde!

I come to this easy conclusion after yesterday's trip to Menton - in a bus crowded to the gills due to the holiday in France and transportation strike in Italy - and today's hike up to the panoramic lookout between Villefranche and Nice. Breathtakingly beautiful!

After traveling down the coast through Cap Ferrat, Beaulieu, Eze, Cap d'Ail, Monaco, past bays and beaches, old villages, cafés, towns with clear Italian influences, I arrive in Menton, a smaller version of Nice, with a long beachfront promenade and unfiltered and ever-present sunshine. It's a symphony of colors and people enjoying themselves.

In the Jean Cocteau Museum, I discover I can get in free with my press pass and take photographs, forbidden others, so enjoy:

http://www.mauiwriter.com/menton

31

The light and lifestyle of this coast lured friends Picasso, Matisse, Cocteau, and others, who often collaborated to celebrate the human spirit. I land for lunch in a charming square, complete with a classical guitar player who brings tears with his rendition of Maleguéna. The Flamenco dancer passes the hat. I enjoy moules et frites (mussels and french fries), un rosé.

The churches are all closed for the holiday, still I hike up to the old town to shoot a few photos, then back down along the seaside. I find a water fountain just when I need it. How can the French make delicious tap water, without a hint of chlorine, when we can't?

The train takes me home. It's starts from Menton with three people, and by the time I get off in Villefranche, it's 8 pm and standing room only.

Yesterday I meet a Scandinavian girl with her mother, waiting for the bus, who tells me about Mt. Boron, so I decide to go this morning and take a bus to the top corniche. "Just turn left after two stop signs; it's only dix minutes," the bus driver tells me. Everyone here uses the term "dix minutes" (ten minutes) to suggest it's a quick walk. Usually it's twenty; this time it's an hour. Uphill. But eucalyptus and jasmine walk with me, and it is enough to breathe the air. Did I mention the killer views of Nice? And Paul Allen's yacht? Elton John's house?

The fort was built on Mont Alban to proffer strategic views of both Nice and Villefranche, so the dukes of Savoy could be on the lookout for pirates, Turks, and French armies. Near the parking lot (yes, most arrive by car), I watch a handful of old men playing boules. When I ask directions to the fort they tell me, "pas loin, madame, dix minutes." (not far, madam, ten minutes.)

At last I reach the fort and views of Villefranche and the coast to the East. Panoramique!

Hiking back to town takes two hours, a few dead-end roads, helpful workers, and a welcomed water fountain. Once back to the vielle ville, I'm hungry, so I stop for saumon grillée et panna cotta at Les Garçons on rue Poilu. The salmon melts in my mouth. The rice is jasmine. The olives are succulent. I realize the food is better because there is less sugar and salt than I'm accustomed to. Lemon gelato taste like lemons. Berries on the panna cotta, like berries, not sugar. Everything creates taste explosions in the mouth. The food also grows here, in this sunny paradise. How could it not be delicious?

Enjoy Mt. Boron and fabulous views of this beautiful coast without the effort, and see if you don't agree that this is the most beautiful coast in the world: http://mauiwriter.com/mtboron

Nice

Villefranche sur Mer

Adieu to the Vielle Ville

Today I whisper aloha and bid adieu to the old town and my sweet apartment at 40 Rue Poilu, in the heart of this historic village. I've been here for two weeks, waking to the sounds of morning, walking its winding streets with stairs and archways, and an occasional fountain, dropping into the boucherie, fromagerie, boulangerie, patisserie, cafés...or walking to the train, the beach, the Wednesday and Saturday markets.

Adieu to new friends Pierre, Bert, Donna, Jean-Charles, Pierre B, Brigitte, Donna, Marie, Thierry, Luca & Federica, Odele, Angela, to my helper at la Poste, my new friend at le petit Casino market.

Adieu to La Grignotiere, Le Mekong, Les Garçons, La Trinquette, Cosmos, duck breast in figs, saumon grillée, tarte tatin, poulet curry, flan des légumes, panna cotta, vins rosé et rouge.

Adieu to St. Michel and St. Pierre, who gives homage to gypsies of Saints Marie's de la Mer by Jean Cocteau, who entreats: "Come yourselves into the structure of the building as living stones."

It's been my joy to be 'home' in the Vielle Ville, here in the heart of picturesque Villefranche Sur

Mer. Tiziano reminds us, *"It's not how far you've traveled, it's what you've brought back."* I'll take the joie de vivre home with me.

Bid adieu with me here
http://mauiwriter.com/vielle

3 Juin

I love this city!

Nice is a city masquerading as a party. Whether invited or simply wandering in, the bar is always open - "café ou vin?" (coffee or wine?) The endless gifts of sun and beach energize this coastal town and raise its already high vibration.

The Grande Dame of the French Riviera - Old town. New places. Parks. Museums. Music. The vibrant Promenade des Anglais. Like the good genes it was born with, Nice never disappoints and always feels like family. The Cours Saleya flower market in the heart of the old town, is a slice of Provence with produce and handicrafts, soaps and perfumes, little outdoor restaurants and big people-watching, and of course lots and lots of flowers from all over Provence.

Ambling through the old town one day, I run into Papayou, a humble little street bistro. Sometimes I just get lucky. My tomato/basil/burratina salad is a full meal, along with crusty French bread and a beautiful red. How can a salad be excellent? It's not just the flavors - tomatoes fresh from Villefranche, burratini from Italy - but the mouth-feel, the perfect slant of a late afternoon sun, friendly and attentive service. Being a bit of a connoisseur, I decide to try their panna cotta. It's the best in Nice, not too hard, not too sweet, just perfect, with a fresh cherry sauce.

Compliments to chef Gillaume. The meal isn't cheap, but I never mind paying for a great experience.

I move to Nice on May 31st, from my large studio in tiny Villefranche to my tiny dorm room in sprawling Nice. It's a tough trip, but three people offer to help: a man on the hill, leaving Villefranche, one young gent, getting on the train, and a woman half my size who sees me struggling and hauls my suitcase down thirty stairs at Nice Ville station. God bless her girl power heart! A quick taxi and I'm checking into my room. We're talking BASIC, but floor to ceiling French doors open over a lovely garden, and it's a block to the Promenade and the beach.

Sana in the front office directs me across the street to a small market that has everything I want: apples, carrots, spinach, oranges, a yam, curry powder, eggs, a baguette, crème fraîche, brie, butter, and a nice Bordeaux Supérieur. Only €19 to fill my whole bag (including wine) There's a small market on every block, which I find much more pleasant than our huge stores. I stop next door at the pharmacie for ibuprofen, and he asks if I want 200 or 400mg. I get a box of 400's (so I can take half as many) for €2.50. Gotta love France!

As the sun sets, I saunter over to the Promenade des Anglais and sit in the sun, people-gazing. All ages and nationalities stroll, jog, skate, rollerblade, bike on this grand passageway. They speak French, Italian, German, Russian, other languages I don't recognize. They laugh, talk, walk in headphones or in silence. The sapphire sea curves east and west, dazzling in the setting sun.

The photos that follow show a bit of La Table Italienne , a delicious display of all things Italian, held over the weekend. There's a long history of Italians here, and they're here still, doing what they do best: olive oil, pasta, truffles, parmigiano and prosciutto, wines and beers, olives, pastries. The tents sprawl along the promenade in the early summer sun and bring Italians, Italian aficionados, and foodies from all over the city and beyond.

Clearly Nice is one of the most beautiful, vibrant cities I've ever experienced. From its stunning coastline to the old town, the center, and beyond, it sparkles and seduces.

Table Italienne:
http://www.mauiwriter.com/tableitalienne

Afterwards I hike up to the old Chateau, where a promontory shows off Nice from both its beach side and its port. There's a money shot in here somewhere.

I'm back in school, enrolled for two weeks in French classes. I ride the bus, since it's across town, €1 (with a 10-pass), takes about fifteen minutes. After initial testing, I'm placed with six others in an intermediate class, which I find pretty intensive. During the morning break I go up to the café on the top floor for petit déjeuner, fresh squeezed orange juice, espresso, and chocolate croissant. The perfect breakfast and only €2.

One of my classmates discovers Gepetto's, where Alex Rici and his wife serve some pretty fabulous Italian food, along with warm Italian hospitality. The scallop ravioli comes with asparagus tips, everything drowning in a mouth-watering sauce, made for a swoon. With a nice Italian red of course.

> *"Mangez bien, riez souvent, aimez beaucoup."*
> *(Eat well, laugh often, love abundantly)*
> popular French saying

Yesterday we got a little briefing after class about Nice and its surrounds, then we walked together through the Vielle Ville. It was educational and extraordinary, complete with gelato.

Dropping by the Museum of Modern and Contemporary Art on my way home, I end up taking more shots of the building than its art.

See it here: MMCA
http://mauiwriter.com/mmca

Enjoy my images of this stunning city
http://www.mauiwriter.com/Nice2

Port poetry

Untethered,
I sit with un verre du vin rosé
And watch the boats
Move on the water.
It ungrounds me.
I feel a floating in my belly
And wonder when I will land.
And who will I be when November comes.

8 Juin

Bonus Sunday . . . a little culture

I'm off to the beach, but I have some photos for you. Just click on the links:

1. **Le Negresco** - the Grande Dame of Nice. I can't afford a room at this splendid hotel, but because "je suis journaliste," I am given access. Enjoy!

http://www.mauiwriter.com/negresco

2. **Palace Messena** - former palace, now a free art and culture museum, showing life in Nice, before and after.

http://www.mauiwriter.com/massena

3. **Musée des Beaux Artes** - in a former private mansion built by a Ukrainian princess, the museum houses a collection of art spanning the past four centuries and includes original works by Nice artists, Rodin, Picasso, and others.

http://www.mauiwriter.com/beauxartes

"Le but de l'art est laver la poussière de la vie quotidienne au large de nos âmes."
(The purpose of art is washing the dust of daily life off our souls.)

Pablo Picasso

10 Juin

On the Street, Sur La Rue 2

Our roving reporter is traveling this month along the Côte d'Azur and asks questions of expats, living in Nice, France:

What's the best and worst of living here as an expat?

Sarah Fausett.
Villefranche sur Mer (from North Carolina). Biologist/geneticist and Student. Here in Nice for 2 months.
"It's frustrating. Hard. Inconvenient. But it's also more fun than doing anything in your comfort zone. It's been a roller coaster. I'm lost and lonely. Then I feel like king of the world. The dichotomy is huge. It's the best social life, mixture of people, easy to mingle. And there are lots of bars, restaurants, things to do. Then there's the bureaucracy. But look out on this bay (Villefranche). I struggle with money but live in one of the richest places on earth. How lucky am I?!!"

Emmett O'Riordan.
Deck hand on yachts. Lives in Nice, from San Francisco (25, parents brought him to France at age 8)

"I love the landscape - from the beach to the mountains, c'est magnifique! I hate the bureaucracy. I like to complain about France but then realize it's my French upbringing that makes me do so (ha-ha)...the French in me. I love the café and wine culture. I'm always meeting amazing people. Recently I was climbing Mont Saint Victoire, literally hanging on the cliff made famous by Cézanne, when I got it - the whole impressionist thing. The French culture is alive!"

Daba Isaac. Senegal.
10 years in Nice.
Secrétaire Generale of AFESEN Commerciale, after graduating from the University of Nice.

"Here one feels a solidarity with tout la monde. People are open, generous, love strangers and foreigners. But it's really expensive. And now there's a growing fear of strangers, of others...maybe taking jobs, changing the French culture. It's a worry."

France Ulrich Reinhold Schele. From Bavaria, here 24 years, 5 months, and 8 days. Non Artist/Non photographer.

"I do naive painting. I make little things. One doesn't need money here for a social life. Everything is outside. I have good friends, but Nice is also a human comedy of negative people...with so many different values. And some people make more money if they don't look for work, since France has a most generous social safety net. Still I'm here."

Elisheva Copin.
Artist/Sculptor.
From Israel (1978)
Elisheva came to France at 26, working as a diplomat in Israeli embassies in Europe and London.
"I loved the new, exciting, modern Europe, so I stayed in Paris and decided to sculpt, which I've done since. One day I realized that children should be raised by the beach. So I moved to Nice. I love the sense of liberty here, but I think some French have become too racist, and sometimes I ponder returning to Israel. Still if the sun's in your heart, you can be happy anywhere."

Antibes and Eze

I didn't want to miss the Picasso Museum, so a couple of friends from school and I rent an electric auto bleue for the day and shoot over to historic Antibes, parking near the beach and hitting the town for food, drink, photographing, and stopping for the indoor and outdoor museum exhibits. The day sparkled as we meandered through streets, worn from centuries of walkers.

At some point Callum thinks we just might have enough charge in the auto to get up to Eze, a little hilltop village we've been told about on campus, so we take the high corniche, landing just as the sun is setting over the coastline. The hotels and restaurants inside the gate are full to overflowing, so we dine in a great little spot just outside the village. Hervé LeFrançois, with his great English and natural humor, takes impeccable care of us at Gascogne Café, and we coast downhill and home to Nice with half a kilometer left on our auto bleue mileage.

15 Juin

Train to Grasse

Caroline (a good friend from school) and I take the train to Grasse, perfume capitol of the world. We actually planned to go to Tende, but missed the bus and didn't want to blow off hours in the train station for the long trip to the mountains, so on to Plan B, Grasse.

It's a quick trip, past the beaches of Cagnes sur Mer, Antibes, Juan des Pins, climbing inland to the old village that Fragonard made famous. Nearly everything in Grasse is Fragonard - the perfumery, museum, restaurants, boutiques...

We taste fabulous aperitifs from the fabulous nougat lady at La Pitchouli, run into a wedding at the church, meander up to the square which overlooks town, then down the winding streets, where we are both called to Le Gazon, a delicious little restaurant, snuggled into a tiny corner of the street. We split a main of mouth-watering lamb with garlic potatoes and a corn flan. But the pièce de résistance is the risotto starter: a perfectly balanced and totally exquisite squid-lemon-basil-parmesan risotto. Hands down best risotto we've ever eaten!

Take a peek at Grasse
http://www.mauiwriter.com/grasse

We hike and bus back to the train station, stopping in Antibes just in time for the Annual Flower Festival and Parade.

Watch it here
http://www.mauiwriter.com/antibesflowerfestival

20 Juin

Loving France

I love the French culture, not just the beautiful old things - fabulous art, medieval towns, ancient churches - but the customs that prevail to this day. The little niceties, the generosity of spirit. It's a polite culture. Greeting each other with kisses and kind words slows things down from the rush I'm used to. Children and men offer seats on the bus and tram. This never happens where I live. Men hug and kiss and not just on football teams. That doesn't happen back home either. I am impressed by these niceties.

One day up at the main square in Villefranche sur Mer, I saunter into a small café, having practiced my French, and ask the Proprietor for three things: un toilette, un café, et wifi (a bathroom, a coffee, and wi-fi). In the nicest possible way he gently corrects me:

"Quatre choses, madame: bonjour monsieur, un toilette, un café, et wifi."

I haven't forgotten. Now from bus drivers to students in my class, I always stop and greet people first. When departing from someone, I always wish them a bon journée, bon soirée - a good day, good evening. It's the French way.

The city of Nice, thanks to an activist mayor, is becoming more green (with the autobleus and velobleus, recycling), more beautiful (with the new central park, better realignments). It's "un ville qui bouge," a city on the move. A dynamic city. Me too...I've never moved more, averaging about seven to eight miles per day on foot. I figure out the secret to French women's trim figures: Bread and café. Three course lunch. Bread and dinner. Tartes. Croissants. Wine. More wine.

Then they walk...everywhere.

The French are efficient. Trains and busses arrive and depart on time, announce the next stop on various transportation methods. Departure and arrival platforms at each station roll on and off at the same level. A week anywhere else and you'll really appreciate French efficiency. And I already mentioned the water - delicious and drinkable. Then there are the prix fixé meals, where appetizer, main course, wine, dessert, and coffee serve up at a very nice price.

I'm becoming a flâneur[5], a connoisseur of the street, getting the art of the stroll down. Whether meandering the streets of old town or along the promenade, I don't rush as was my custom. At a certain pace, thoughts vanish, and all that's left is the holiness of the ordinary, the experience of the moment, le joie de vivre.

I'm also learning how to nap. They do siestas here. Shops close midday for a couple of hours. I don't know if it's the Italian influence or the sun, or just human need, but it's a great tradition ...along with all the little kindnesses: a limoncello from a friendly café owner following a fun conversation, the waiter who tries to fix a single man up with me when offering him a table, the old gent squeezing past me on the bus, 'a bit close' he says in French, smiling broadly. His flirt puts a smile on my face and makes the whole crowded trip go better.

I call Guillaume and his bike taxi to move me from one residence to another, across town. E10 is the quote, but he goes out of his way, down the

---

[5] Flâneur (pronounced: [flɑnœʁ]), from the French noun flâneur, means "stroller", "lounger", "saunterer", or "loafer". Flânerie refers to the act of strolling, with all of its accompanying associations. The flâneur was, first of all, a literary type from 19th century France, essential to any picture of the streets of Paris. The word carried a set of rich associations: the man of leisure, the idler, the urban explorer, the connoisseur of the street. The flâneur has become an important symbol for scholars, artists and writers. (Road Scholar)

Promenade, stopping for photos, pointing out the dedication this year of a small Statue of Liberty, erected to commemorate the Americans who liberated France. Then he bikes a few blocks out of his way to show me the lamps on the Opera House, also designed by Gustave Eiffel, architect of the Tower of his name in Paris and the Statue of Liberty in New York City. Overall I get a forty-minute ride for a ten minute trip, full of information and friendship.

The Albanian waiter, the French chef and Thai proprietor, the Senegalese Ambassador, so many others - they each exhibit a patience with me, a certain warmth. These kindnesses are not lost on me. Gently I am learning to slow down, to be enriched by people and places, all so beneficent. France speaks sweetly to me, and I learn to see what I don't yet know, to see as vibration (like the impressionists), rather than language or concept...or thought. It's a beautiful, rich culture. It's seductive and alive. And I am thoroughly enchanted by it.

"On ne voit bien qu'avec le cœur."
(One sees well only with the heart)
Le Petit Prince by Antoine de Saint Exupéry

23 Juin

Genoa, a little side trip to Italy

Good friends from back home email me saying they are in Venice, heading to Vernazza in a few days. "Join us," they insist. So I search online for a place, find one (if I can switch rooms during my stay), and head south by train to Genoa, where I stay for two days, until my room opens up in Vernazza. My heart beats faster on the train, as I fly past beaches and little farms. Italy! So much in us wants the familiar - places, friends. But there's a quickening that happens when I'm alone on the road. I'll admit it. I'm a travel junkie. Meanwhile I switch over from French to Italian. Buongiorno. Grazie.

Quintessential Italy, birthplace of Christopher Columbus, blue jeans, and the lotto, a city of 1.6 million, Genoa bustles. It's noisy and robust, from architecture to transport, fashion to food.

I land in the Centro Historico in my Mini Hotel, which at €25 per night is the best housing value of my trip so far. After three and a half hours on trains from Nice, and a quick taxi to my hotel, I head out to amble the alleyways, then catch the football game at a little trattoria. It comes with a beautiful pasta and a Barolo.

As the sky mutes, I watch lovers enjoying the city and each other. I want that - the look, the embrace, joy with another. But being alone means moments like this - the thrill of the game, shared with more great wine...and five gorgeous guys.

I only have one more day in Genoa, so I start early, explore piazzas, churches, and Mt. Belvedere, which you get to by elevator. At the top of the world, there's a killer view of this sprawling, rambunctious port city.

A beautiful lunch is served by a beautiful Italian. He brings little bruschettas with pomodora and mozzarella. And a very nice Barbera. With a creamy, dark Belgian chocolate gelato to finish. Go for the eye candy. Stay for the gelato. Ciao Bella!!

Here are some images of Genoa
http://www.mauiwriter.com/genoa

Vernazza & the Cinque Terre
3 Vignettes:

I

I land in room 2 at Gianni Franzi, with a balcony looking out to sea, up exactly 100 old, weathered stone steps from the piazza. I get lost later, making my way back to the room with bags of fruit, water, wine. Lost for twenty minutes on old stairways and back alleyways, climbing (and climbing), viewing a box of geraniums here, a Madonna and bougainvilleas on the wall there, just enough to think I'm in familiar territory. Then I realize I AM LOST.

I was mapless coming down via train from Nice and the (now familiar) French coast into Italy. San Remo, Savina...where am I? Am I close?? I come to rely on the kindness of strangers. At Portofino I begin a quiet anticipation, remembering an earlier stay in that uniquely charming town years before. After passing Portofino, everything gets better - little villages, hill towns, beaches. At Levante I jump off and into a waiting train to La Spezia, grabbing a E1 onion focaccia (fabulous Italian bread, smothered in caramelized onions). Shortly thereafter, I disembark at Vernazza.

So much of this trip has felt disjointed like this. Too much unknown, too little planned, a stretch of adventure, pure and true, as we adventure junkies like it. My life too now is mapless. Having left my last home permanently, I am on the road, letting each day, each week, take me where it will. It is enough. It is more than enough.

I take my cameras for a walk around the village of Vernazza, one 'money shot' after another, the beauty felt to my core. Rumi reminds us to *"live life as though everything is rigged in your favor."* It is sweet to live with such grace.

By 9 am the village comes alive. Delivery trucks bring goods via a tight street, open to certain vehicles only until 9:30 am. Shopkeepers hang their wares out to entice tourists; fishermen head out on their boats or toss a line from the rocks; tour skiffs jockey for position; and everyone gathers for espresso. The bell tower chimes loud and long.

Following the thunder of this morning's storm, I am back in my room, reading Ruth Reichel's *Delicious!* when the bell rings at one o'clock, and I remember I have an unfinished pizza from the night before - artichokes, mozzarella, pesto...on a thin crust. Benissimo! I open a bottle of red, recommended by the shopkeeper in the Enoteca up from the piazza. It smells of the stairs leading to the bell tower but tastes like currants and blackberries, all rich and earthy and dark like a wine cellar in Calcinara. Re de Peiu, Golfo dei Poeti, Rosso 2010. It's almost too good for lunch, but it's Italy, so I indulge.

Indulge yourself - enjoy Vernazza!

http://www.mauiwriter.com/vernazza

II

By afternoon the dark skies clear, the sun is strong, and I decide to hike the hill that leads out of town along the path towards Monterosso al Mare. The Cinque Terre is a special landscape, unique in the world, with a rich history in the region of Liguria, and declared a UNESCO World Heritage Site in 1997. In 1999 the National Park of the Cinque Terre and its Protected Marine Area (enlarged in 2004) were instituted, bonding the five towns of the area. Today tourists come to experience sustainable tourism, hiking the wine trails above the towns, and staying to experience the rich cultures and gastronomy of Vernazza, Monterosso al Mare, Corniglia, Manarola, and Riomaggiore.

Ferries and trains transport tourists and locals from town to town. Spend some time here, and get on Cinque Terre time. It's been discovered, but if you stay awhile, you can make your own discoveries. Get to know the people, the birds, stones, cloud formations, which focaccia you like the best, which prosecco. Gianni, Michela, Alessandro...and the experiences that make the Cinque Terre come alive for you.

Enjoy the Cinque Terre
http://www.mauiwriter.com/cinqueterre

III

In the morning birds own the cliff. People gather on terraces for breakfast and forget for awhile their cares of the day, lost in watching gulls soar and sweep, listening to waves crashing below, caught up in the magic fusion of sea and sky and a horizon in deep contrast as far as the eyes travel.

As fate would have it, I head up the main street to the Blue Marlin Bistro. I have skyped Emily to meet there, hoping she has wifi somewhere and gets my messages. As I arrive, before finding a table, I look up towards the train station and see my friend Kate, lugging her suitcase down the stairs. We greet with hugs then find their B&B up another back alleyway, then head out for a bite. I end up with a bad excuse for a caprèse salad, but am happy to be with friends, sharing travel stories...in English.

After finishing a bottle of wine on my terrace, we're back at the Blue Marlin for the France-Equador playoff game, along with the two daughters from Georgia I'd met earlier. During six weeks in France I met two North Americans. Here only one day along the Cinque Terre and they're everywhere. I begin to miss France.

◇

We girls need a beach day, so we head to Monterosso by train. It's late, we miss the first train, the second never arrives, and we wait for over an hour then smash into an over-crowded train...for a 3-minute trip. It's worth the wait :-) We settle into beach chairs and order a walnut-stuffed pasta and beer. The sun plays peek-a-boo for an hour or two as beach vendors target us. We get used to saying "no, grazie, ciao."

When the sun finally blasts through, we swim and sun, and enjoy another beer. At dusk we'll walk into the historic town for appel spritzers, a local favorite, and dinner, before taking the train 'home' to Vernazza.

Beach Day at Beautiful Monterosso al Mare
http://www.mauiwriter.com/monterosso

The Italian team loses, and everyone in town is on a bummer for a day or two. Italian fans take their football very seriously.

After climbing above the town on the path south, I sit for a fresh oj, watching swimmers below navigate the waves at 'secret beach'. In the afternoon, I interview some of the people who make Vernazza work.

Sulla Strada, 3

Gianni Franzi - hotel, café, bar, restaurant, wine label. Opening his first (and Vernazza's first) trattoria in 1964 with his mom, Gianni is clearly the business grandfather of Vernazza, overseeing a small empire, leaning heavily on a dedicated staff of twenty employees. His was the only restaurant in town until fifteen years ago.

"Rick Steves actually put us and the Cinque Terre on the map 25 years ago. Since then we've enjoyed a growing tourist market. The season used to be mid June to mid September, but it now extends at least seven months of the year, April through October. Of course marketing is so much easier now with the internet, so we're full all the time. We use social media to big advantage, and fill up with lots of Americans."

Note: Vernazza is full of Americans, and English is spoken everywhere.

Direct flights to Pisa help deliver guests to Gianni's doorstep. Or steps, as the case may be. Most rooms are between 80 and 100 steps up from the Piazza Marconi, the heart of Vernazza.

I was lucky enough to get a room (actually two, having had to switch after three days due to a prior booking) among the 24 he controls. I am delighted with the room, the service, and the marvelous location, overlooking the coastline.

"I'm a lucky man. I live where I work (actually up on the top, with a garden and my lemon trees). Every penny I made I put back into the business, expanding over the years. I haven't done much new recently, just renovating all the time. My son Emanuele runs the restaurant. My sister-in-law Marchela handles a great deal. Everyone does their job really well, so my job now is easy." (smiles)

My Scandinavian girlfriend of twenty years adds all the quotes and artistic touches. Most of our kitchen help is Moroccan, Alessandro handles the Wine tasting, and I hired a friend, former professor from Pisa to work my vineyards and create the Biancas and Rosso of our private label."

Gianni leaves the room for a moment, and a staff member brings out his white and red wines. The

Rosso is wonderful. Earthy, with a Cinque Terre nose like terraces and the cave to the sea. It's a blend of refosco del peduncolo rosso with 10% cabernet sauvignon, and 5% syrah, oaked one year.

Shortly winemaker, Bartolo Lercari and Danish girlfriend Lise Bertiim arrive. Bartolo's family has been in winemaking his whole life, and he's been at  it 17 years. He produces 7,500 bottles a year, but he's noticed the climate changing. They now pick earlier, compared to 30 years ago - the first two weeks in September for the whites and about a month later for reds.

"The reflection of the light from the sea helps the growing. Salt in the air creates a challenge, but plants have to suffer a little. (smiles) We have a wonderful team of ladies who work the vineyards. By caring for the vines and the terraces, we have the means to do the work of restoration for our region of the Cinque Terre."

Gianni commands the best businesses and locations in town. He says it best:

"I was born and raised here. I work here with my family and friends. I'm a lucky man."

Gianni Franzi, Vernazza (lodging and restaurant)
www.giannifranzi.it
info@giannifranzi.it
0039-0817-821003

"The nose seduces.
Legs film inside the glass.
And the taste -
berries, tannin, deep woods.
Sunshine. Earth."
Gascon Malbec

 Flavio Malagamba,
Shopkeeper - Souvenirs
Born and raised in
Vernazza, Flavio opens
daily at 8 am and stays
open til 7 pm, taking full
advantage of tourists here
for the Cinque Terre. He
works every day himself
and has two employees.

"We had a couple of bad years after 2008, but tourists are back, and business is good."

Michela Basso, Ristorante Belforte In 1965 Michela's father started this wonderful restaurant on the point. Michela took it over eight years ago, managing eleven employees and a kitchen staff of five, serving up a fabulous dining experiences at lunch and dinner for visitors and locals alike. They took a hit during the economic collapse of 2008 and the flood of 2011, but Michela feels lucky that they've rebounded well, serving more meals now than ever, ninety on the terraces and twenty-four inside. She groans at the 60-70% taxes she pays, but her enormous success helps. Like so many others who run businesses here, Michela grew up in Vernazza and is a child of the Cinque Terre. *"It's a special place, and we are all lucky to be here."*

After tasting the food and experiencing the impeccable service, I think luck has little to do with it. Belforte is one of the many experiences that make the Cinque Terre come alive.

Ristorante Belforte
www.ristorantebelforte.it/en
info@ristorantebelforte
0039-0187-812-222

Alessandro Villa,
Vernazza Wine Experience
At 5 pm, six days a week, the upper deck at
Gianni Franzi's opens for wine tasting with
Alessandro, certified sommelier. Another spin-
off opportunity from the Gianni empire. Now
thatsa howa to do a wine tasting! Not to mention
the location, hanging on a cliff over the sea.

Asking your wine preferences, Alessandro
chooses a selection, perfectly fit for your tastes.
Here's what I experience (along with generous
nibbles of nuts, vegetables, grana padano
cheese):

1. Prosecco. La Farrah - Valdobbiadene -
Prosecco Superiore. Excellent! Dry, Light, fresh,
finely bubbled. Perfectly balanced. Gooseberries
and early kiwis.

2. Rubico - Lacrima (tears) di Mollo d'Alba
The nose of roses is remarkable, its taste not at all rosy, but light and different.
3. Elena - Sarotto Barbara d'Alba (Piedmont). Earthy. Stones from the hillside. Caves and berries. It transports. *"Meditation wine."*
4. Then an aperitif - Vermouth del professore. Antica Rigetta

Opened in April 2014, this small business is a huge success already. The new deck and a friendship with Gianni created the business opportunity, along with Alessandro's fine entrepreneurial spirit.

Doing research for the European Commission on the Ligurian Region, Villa was born in Genoa and raised in Vernazza, living along the Cinque Terre for 20 years. Long a supporter of the Save Vernazza organization and a former professor at the University of Turin, teaching sustainable tourism and development, Alessandro is first to admit the difference between academic discussion of the problems/solutions and reality.

"We had to rebuild after the flood of 2011, but the tourists are back in droves and now pose a threat to this ecosystem they come to visit and save. The worst are the trainloads of excursions from Florence and other major Italian cities. They descend like hoards through our town. It's good for business but difficult for our fragile region."

"The Cinque Terre is a sanctuary whose coastline was uninhabited until the 11th or 12th century, when a few families began growing wines, olives, chestnuts, and mulberries (for silk). In 1944 we were Nazi-occupied and bombed by the Allies. Our economic boom began in the 50's and 60's, and in 1997 the Cinque Terre was made a UNESCO World Heritage site, then a National Park. Today the Cinque Terre has about 1,000 residents - 600 in Vernazza, 300 in Corniglia, and about 100 above town. St. Marguerita is our patron saint."

"I wanted to create a place where people could drink well. Australians and Californians know wines, and I love to expose them to varieties they'll remember."

He's done it. Outstanding wines, service, and location makes this an exceptional experience.

Alessandra (Professor Villa) has written a book, *Vernazza - Cinque Terre, a guide:* restaurants, lodging, history of the area and the sanctuary (land and sea), more about wines of the region, and typical Vernazza and Italian food and recipes. Buy the book.

> Vernazza Wine Experience, Cinque Terre
> www.cinqueterrewinetasting.com
> info@cinqueterrewinetasting.com
> 00 39 331 3433801

More on the Cinque Terre:
http://www.parconazionale5terre.it/?id_lingue=2

1 Juin to 11 Juillet

Trip Diary, Vernazza to Vence

Raw diary:
31 Juin - Travel day: three trains and a bus. Up the Italian coast and back to France - Vernazza to Monterosso to Genoa to Ventimiglia to Nice to Cagnes sur Mer to Vence (8 am to 7 pm).

Police board at Ventimiglia, moving through the train and getting off with six young men, before the train moves on. Immigration is an issue all over the world, and with so many coming from Yemen and other northern African and Middle Eastern countries into Italy, the French guard their border at Ventimiglia.

I finally connect with Tony and Jane, the Brittish residents also staying at the guest house I booked through a friend. Without being able to use my French tele in Italy and with no phones for sale in Vernazza, communications have been very sparse, and I'm nervous, arriving without being able to reach anyone.

Note: WhatsApp works for texting in Europe if you can get on wifi.

After a long travel day I'm landed in Vence. I grab a glass of wine and moules et frites (default meal) while waiting at La Victoire in the square, right outside Vence's old town. As it darkens, between nine and ten pm, waiter Paschal finally gives me a map of the historic village, drawing a red line to my street, and I haul my suitcase and backpack through the cobbled streets of the old town, finding my way. I knock, but no one responds. At last Tony arrives, guiding me to my room two floors up. I sleep, exhausted.

1 Juillet - By eight am I'm on the square with a cappuccino and pain chocolate (chocolate croissant). I drop in the Poste to add minutes to my French tele (yep, it's one of those). The market is filled with bountiful fruits and vegetables. I take my food treasures home, unpack my suitcase, then head back out for a leisurely walk. Flậneur. Then I nap from one to three, finishing my photo editing by seven. Dinner at Le Clemenceau (Tony mentions it has the best and fastest wifi). I meet and photo the

waitresses, Sissi and Julie, then get on with a filet mignon in noisette sauce, veggie flan, pommes, a nice red. Tres bon! But too much, so I take half my dinner home. This is so unFrench.

2 Juillet - St. Paul de Vence with Tony and Jane. Share coffee and conversation. I buy a fresh green juice from Sylvie on the square, then proceed to walk the city on the hill. At the first art gallery I get into a lively discussion with Julien, who reminds me not to miss the Luberon and his favorite town, Les Baux de Provence. I decide to add it to my study of Les Villàges Perché (medieval hill towns). I stroll about the old town, shoot dozens of photos.

Enjoy this slideshow of St. Paul de Vence
http://www.mauiwriter.com/stpauldevence

The bus back to Vence leaves at 15:20. I enjoy salad greens and left over filet mignon for early supper, with the wine Tony & Jane left for me.

Note: There are dogs everywhere (on leashes), yet I've seen only one poop in seven weeks! (in Nice). Is it the free bag dispensaries? Habit? Just good French manners?

3 Juillet - It's a quiet day photo editing, writing, catching up Italy and Vernazza for my blog and Facebook. After saying aloha to Tony and Jane, I hike the old, narrow stairs to the top floor to do some laundry...and enjoy expansive views and a magnificent sunset on the top deck.

To Do:
Send FR n IT notes
Edit photos and upload 3 slide shows
Write and post blog, 3 vignettes
Translate Mathieu - write back
Write Susan & Phil - in Poyols, Luc, Die
Text Callum to connect with bag he's storing for
    me in Nice
I take a little walk about. Wifi @ Clemenceau.

4 Juillet - my boyfriend comes tonight from Nice.
I shop for food, prep la maison et le lit (the house
and the bed). I try to nap, knowing it will be a
long night :-)

> *Il n'y a qu' un bonheur dans la vie,*
> *c'est d'aimer et d'être aimé.*
> (There is only one happiness in life:
> to love and be loved)
> Georges Sand

5 Juillet - Wake @ 7. M sleeps til 9:30. We take a
bus together to Cagnes sur Mer, where he
catches the train back to Nice, and I visit the
Chateau and Museum Grimaldi, enjoying both
the disturbing images of torture and the
panoramic views from the top deck. Dejeuner at
le Village Brasserie in the square is poulet rôti
avec salade et frites. I take home nearly half a
chicken so that I can enjoy tarte de pomme avec
chantilly et berries. Cindy gives excellent and
friendly service.

It's a long, hot, uphill hike to Renoir's home, now an amazing museum property. Once there, I'm transported. Inspired. Hang out for a couple of hours. (more @ this sensational experience later)

Then I bus home to Vence, stopping at Le Clemenceau, where I've discovered pastis. Actually Tony introduced me to it on their last night in town. Oh dear. It's perfect for a sore throat, following too much vocal excitement at recent World Cup games. When you don't want a beer or wine, when you want to save E1 over a Perrier, it's only €2.50 and all the water you can drink. Plus I sleep really well.

6 Juillet - Home. M texts, asks if I liked the watermelon he left. I think of Pablo Neruda and his ode...and painting, hanging in my kitchen. I would write poetry for M if I thought he'd understand. He brings me food, cooks for me, uncracks a shell, toughened over time. Texts me sweet...and dirty. Has no idea of my value, yet values me anyway. I like his strangeness, his sweetness, the difficulties with language, the humor, the niceties. His transparency. His mystery.

7 Juillet - Still troubled by not being able to unlock my iPhone (apple!!$@&%#*!), so using 2 phones - the French one for local calls & texts, the iPhone for email, FB, google translate, surfing, etc., but I have no wifi in the house, so I hang at Le Clemenceau & La Victoire - where Paschal and the owner have fun with me...and

rock American music!
Wifi code: zephirienne241269

Garçon Giovanni refuses to serve me lunch. I've been working for about two hours over un café, then decide to order lunch. When he looks sideways at me, I suggest he set up the place next to me, and I'll jump over to eat.

"Why don't you finish your work, madame, and I'll set you up a nice table on the terrace?"

How American to work right through lunch. How French to stop and actually enjoy the meal, which of course I do: salmon cooked to perfection, cauliflower flan, zucchini, rice. Côte white. Café.

I take my ordinateur (computer) home, grab a one-hour nap, then take my camera back out for a walk around the old city in the late afternoon, with the soft sunlight photographers love. I see a beautiful young boy, standing in an open doorway and ask if I can take his picture.

Ali Bouchareb, with his great hair and tee shirt and fast fingers, takes my iPhone to type in his name, after I stumble a couple of times. He's adorable, about ten, striking with his platinum tips  on black hair, wearing a t-shirt that reads "take me as I am."

8 Juillet - Café and wifi at Ristorante Clemenceau. Meet Luca. Bank machine refuses both cards. Mon dieu!! My bank has frozen my account without notice. Or reason.

People sweep the streets - jobs and less noise pollution. Actually people work all over France in jobs we rarely see back home, where so much is done by machine. Or left undone.

Another World Cup game tonight. Brazil and Germany.

I check in with Mirabelle to pick up my sewing. Head via bus back to St. Paul to visit the Musée Fondation Maecht. It's awesome! (more later) Stop at the Soeurs (Sisters') Hermitage on my way down the hill. It is so lovely, with sunshiny terraces growing grapes, vegetables, and flowers, a courtyard by the living compound, a sweet old church. Makes me want to be a nun.

9 Juillet - Buy big fancy heirloom tomatoes and fresh basilica at street market. Stop in little patisserie for "croissant ou pain?" Lady remembers me from the buratta I bought at the Italian shop yesterday, suggests a half loaf (E.45) I make my way home and make the best salad ever, with a crusty French bread and fleurs de basilica (basil flowers)...and the buratta, purchased from Francesco. Eat on the top deck, looking over the mountains - a picture perfect day, 78 degrees, filled with sunshine. More laundry, house cleaning. Without being able to use the bank machines, I'm now short of funds to leave for Andrea. Will have to send. Or I can Paypal her friend, who will see her next week.

Tonight's the big game: Netherlands/Argentina. A gibbous moon rises over Le Clemenceau. I am with friends. Pastis. Happy.

10 Juillet
To do:
Ck currencies $1.35/.73
E Nice expats piece to editor
E to Peter. Might have to come visit. Save $$.

Ck cheap Greek room near beach, P&D
Yes to Cannes apt - $1300/cash. (call bank)
Trip advisor - La Victoire, Rosarie, etc.
Upload Grimaldi & Renoir & St. Paul slide shows
E Pics to Tony n Jane
Test blog.com/fr
Upload fr vignettes
Write CsM blog
St Paul photos
Finalize French Culture piece and pick a few
    photos - Statue of Liberty. Culture. Tram
FB pics/blog - new pics
Text M - wish him a good Ramadan
Call David, back from UK

Hike up to Chapelle Rosarie (Matisse's chapel) C'est fermé. Walk home. Stop for lunch from Samuel at Bistro du Peyra, by the fountain. Moules á la Gorgonzola et frites. Vin rosé. Café.

Rain. I slip rounding corner from main square (3x a charm - ouch/knee - again). Smash iPhone (yea screen protectors). Need shoes with grip. No tread left on flip flops.

Recharge phone then head back out, hoping for a bus to the Chapelle. No luck. Stop at Orange shop - no screen protectors. Removes mine. Protectors are worth every penny!

Quel Disappointment!! (Rosarie Chapelle) After feeling welcomed throughout the south of France at over 25 museums, many free (and ALL churches), I thought €6 for this experience was a rip. No handouts or information. No taking photos. A 10-minute talk in the Chapelle (en français), a walk through a hallway filled with posters of other Matisse exhibits, and a small postcard/bookstore. 'Goodbye, madame.' No views. No gardens, which from the outside had looked enticing. Several attendants remind me that this is "privée" so not run for the benefit of guests, but for profits only. I feel it. I don't mind paying for a good experience, but even E6 is too much for a bad one. Matisse's work saved this from being a zero, but even he would hate what it's become.

I stop on the way home at the old stone water works and Chapelle des Penitents Blancs, built in the 17th century and my favorite local church.

They're setting up the main square for big music events to come...every night throughout the month. Plays. Songs. Judo exhibits. I might make it back for Pink Martini. Note: We need a commons back home. It's a community builder!

David, who hooked me up with Andrea's Vence pad, meets me for a rosé and catch up, later some pasta at Italian spot outside the west gate.

11 Juillet - All week I've been very conscious of how much I NEED SUN AND SUNLIGHT! Here in the old town, the home is sandwiched on four levels between other homes, so there's light on the top floor and deck, but it's progressively darker down to my room (2nd), living/kitchen

(1st), and basement. Still, with all the travel, I love settling in, cooking, dancing, nesting.

I'm off today to Cannes, after stopping in La Victoire to bid adieu to Paschal et al, steeling myself with a great espresso for the moving day ahead. I hope my new place is sweet, with lots of light and a sea view.

Walking to the bus stop outside of town, the tomato lady at the market recognizes me, gives me a large, fleshy apricot as an aloha gift, wishes me 'bon voyage'.

Note: Lots of children here. Everywhere. Not so much in Ashland.

The bus drops me off within a block of La Gare in Cagnes sur Mer. I buy my own ticket at the French machine, remembering when I couldn't. Assenseurs, yea! 60-minute wait and two late/missed trains. Talk with old worker dix minutes en français. Cool breeze. I'm a patient traveler.

Enjoy these photos of Vence
http://www.mauiwriter.com/vence

ℭhree ℭreasures

FONDATION MAEGHT
A stunning collection, a force of nature, the mighty Maeght Foundaton Musée celebrates its 50th anniversary this summer.

Whether you love modern art or not, do not miss this French treasure! Tucked away in the hills above the Côte d'Azur by St Paul de Vence, you will find works by Chagall, Matisse, Braque, Kandinsky, Giacometti, Calder, Klee, Leger, Bonnard, Kelly, Miro, the big names of the modern movement.

Sculptures hang out in gardens and waterfalls, then grace the studios where famous art joins them. The architectural structure is a work of modern art itself. Extraordinaire, with views (beyond the art) of the mountains and the sea, this entire place inspires.

"Il me baisera des baisers de sa bouche;
oui, tes entreintes dont meilleures que le vin."
(he kisses me with his mouth...sweeter than wine)
Chagall

Go! (link here)
http://www.mauiwriter.com/maecht

CHATEAU MUSÉE GRIMALDI

Built in 1300 as a fort, transformed in 1620 into a palace, acquired by the city of Cagnes sur Mer in 1937 and made into a museum and in 1948 a historic monument, the museum today houses contemporary art exhibits. The top deck has 360 degree views from the mountains to the sea. The images in the show were intense and disturbing.

See if you don't agree...
http://www.mauiwriter.com/grimaldi

◊

RENOIR MUSÉE

I take a bus down from the chateau then walk uphill 'dix minutes' to Les Collettes, entering the property from the lower gardens. I am instantly transported to an earlier time and imbued with the soft light that launched the Impressionist movement, infusions of eucalyptus and pine, a jumble of flowers, views of the chateau below across fields and sprawling trees. I lie in the shade, listening to cicadas, nearly overwhelmed with scent overload. Colors sizzle in the midday sun. Birds and butterflies fly and flit. I listen to it all, along with the quiet.

At 2 pm, following the obligatory two-hour lunch break, I enter the house, filled with original Renoirs, photographs of his time here (with occasional friends Modigliani, Rodin, Bonnard, Matisse) during for the last twelve years of his life. If I lived here, I'd paint too. Big, sensual splotches of color on canvas. Like Renoir.

ENJOY!
http://www.mauiwriter.com/renoir

11 Juillet

Cannes

Corrine meets my train, picks me up in her Mercedes. She's petite, blonde, adorable. An accountant by profession. Her son has booked me online, and the rental is a family affair. She takes me to the tiny studio in Le Suquet, with great views of the port and sea. We share some of the chilled rosé she left for me (a common touch in vacation rentals here). I unpack then walk up the hill. There's a church on top. Everywhere in France there's so much reverence for the Mother. The Musée de la Castre is filled with history, and outside, the views are electrifying.

At La Farigoule I enjoy fried zucchini flowers with a spicy aioli, fresh filet of dorade with basil, zucchini. It's a late lunch/early dinner at 4:30, finished off with Orange Wine - blood oranges with rosé et canelle (vanilla). It's delicious and marks the end of another long travel day.

As I unpack and settle in, I stand at my open windows, loving the sea breeze. The beach across the bay turns golden with the setting sun, and another full moon rises over Cannes. I am filled with joy.

The more I follow my bliss, the more it seems to follow me.

◇

July is filled with discovery - new foods, beaches, exhibits, museums, towns, friends. Sarah and Jake take the train from Villefranche. Callum and girls visit from Nice. I meet new comrades in Cannes...and Vence, Mougins, Cannet, Biot. Germany wins the cup over Argentina.

Navigating through Le Suquet (Cannes old town), Rue Meynadier is a slice of life, a big little street with all kinds of shops, dozens of restaurants, street musicians, tourists and locals, enjoying their days and nights.

The music is remarkable...on the street, at dinner, in the clubs. I come to love the weekly pyrotechnics, hosted by various countries, choreographed with music. I watch the fireworks from my lookout in my little apartment in the

Suquet. Every single week it's a half hour of pure joy!

I'm loving Cannes, filled with happy souls and great shopping, from food to fashion. The busses take off a block from my studio, and the train is a ten minute walk, so getting around the Côte is uncomplicated and fun. Then there's the Croisette and the best people-watching ever.

Early on I discover Salsamenteria Di Parma, a new eatery on the scene (Rue Meynadier), where Brando (from Milano), pours me a big bowl of Lambrusco, while serving up yummy breads with a variety of spreads - roasted red pepper, artichoke, parma. I order the anolini, stuffed baby raviolis - little pillows of heaven. With fresh parmigiano of course. Café. Panna cotta, with fraises (strawberries). Brando entreats me to "come again," as he gives me a little card for a free prosecco. "Wine's on me next time," he flirts.

I discover a new patisserie at Marché Forville and meet Marc and Jessica, who speak great English, help me order. I become a regular, stopping in for my baguette, a croissant, little sweet treats.

Cannes is more Italian than Nice, and Italian is spoken everywhere. Still it's weird hearing Chinese and Africans speak French. Perfectly.

Mooji whispers: *"Know this. When you say 'I', the true meaning of 'I' is joy, it is happiness, it is life...and it's also the witnessing of life. Enjoy what comes, but don't worry about anything at all. Just be happy happy happy. Know that whatever happens in life, the final point: everything's fine, all is fine. Namasté."*

I am happy. I photograph. I write. I blog. I eat more pasta and drink more wine than ever before. I'm thinking of writing a book on how to do France on €100 per day (ha ha). I bus to the industrial zone (Les Tourrades) for better shoes, a fantastic saumon grillé et rosé at a workingman's café. Day tripping on Isle St. Marguerite, I hike the island and lose myself in my lenses. Then I jump in the Mediterranean and swim a mile.

In the evening, friends join me for champagne and hors d'œuvre of duck confit paté, cheeses, grapes, figs, the little French radishes I've come to love. After great conversations, we head out for jazz and other live music in the Suquet. Drinks and dessert. Comme il faut.

At l'Escale bord du Mer, I watch a kid tease his sister, and two old Frenchmen engage in deep conversation. A great joy floods over me. Just to be here now, in the human condition, with fellow travelers. It is enough. C'est une bonne vie.

20 Juillet

Cloudy with a chance of Biot

Sunday I get up, ready for a beach day, but alas it's cloudy. First I've seen in awhile, so instead I decide to train and bus to Biot, a little hill town recommended by friends. Since I'm doing a story on Le Villàges Perché, it's a no brainer.

The train leaves on time and without a hitch. At the bus stop in Biot sur Mer, I meet Kenza, a chef from Paris, here on vacation. She sorts out the directions to the vielle ville, then invites me for a fabulous meal next time I'm in Paris. She speaks French for 'dix minutes', and I understand every word.

Her bus comes then I'm waiting with six fun-loving Britts, and we share and laugh for thirty minutes until the bus finally comes (slow Sunday schedule), taking us uphill. Biot is known for its glass blowing, ceramics, and the Museum of Ferdnand Leger, a giant in the modern art movement.

By serendipity I find my way down a little side street and am warmly welcomed by Eric at Le Jarrier, where I enjoy a lovely view, sweet breeze, nice jazz, excellent food, and impeccable service - lunch as only the French do.

Every great meal has a good story. An amuse bouche of watermelon pieces and bruschetta with tapenade et aioli is followed by an asparagus salad with petite mozzarella, olives, tomatoes, greens and fennel. Lightly dressed. Lamb with wild mushrooms, a summer vegetable flan (light as a breeze), frites. How can I be eating so much (and so well) and losing weight? Two glasses of a wonderful local red are included. Café (naturellement) et après - white rum with three raisins. If you're ever in Biot, treat yourself.

I run into the Britts again at a lookout. And again at the glass-blowing guild. And again on the last bus. We're still laughing. They lift my spirits on this long and overcast day.

Enjoy Biot
http://www.mauiwriter.com/biot

One of the best things about travel is the people you meet along the way.

22 Juillet

Le Cannet — a pleasant surprise!

Following my morning trip to Marché Forville, I'm off to the Musée Bonnard. The women at the bus station recommend it, advise to take bus number 1 to Cannett, which drops me off right across the street from the museum.

Opened in 2011 to honor the famed Cannet artist, the museum houses many Pierre Bonnard masterpieces, especially landscapes, inspired by his adopted town.

"During my morning walks, I amuse myself by defining various concepts of landscapes - landscape, intimate landscape, decorative landscape, etc. But each day I take in different elements - the sky, the objects, everything is constantly changing. One could end up drowning in it. But it enables us to live."
            Pierre Bonnard, 1940

Les Belles Endormies (Sleeping Beauties) is the current collection of paintings, drawings, and sculptures (from museums and private collections) It's compelling and features Bonnard, Brancusi, Matisse, Picasso, Renoir, Maillol, Van Dongen, Vuillard, other masters. Caught in that magic suspension of time (sleeping, resting, dreaming), these femmes showcase the formidable talent of artistic greats in the late 1800's and early 1900's. By the fourth floor I'm thinking that the models have all fallen asleep, and I need a coffee. It's a stunning show!

Elle est belle comme ceux qui n'ont pas souffret...
Seulement un peu pâle d'avoir depuis cent ans
sommeille sans les arbres, sans voir le ciel.
(She is beautiful like those that have not suffered ...
Only a little pale to have a hundred years
slumbers without trees, without seeing the sky)

"Je reve, donc je suis"
(I dream, therefore I am)
August Strindburg

Femme Couchée, 1932 - Pablo Picasso

I wander the gardens and notice the church next door, the Eglise Sainte Philomene. Later sauntering up a small street, I find (surprise!) a square overlooking the church, the museum, and the entire Cannes coastline.

The old village is a surprise and a treat. After a chocolate glacé, I take 'Bonnard's promenade' and enter the artist's universe - a cultural stroll to eight sites throughout town, all painted by Bonnard and marked by his images.

Ubiquitous to every French town is a war memorial to those lost in 1st and 2nd world wars. I stand at each, saddened by the "children of" - Cannet...Biot...Mougins...Vence...Nice...EVERY town, killed by national violence.

I watch children playing netless volleyball in a park, enjoy all the painted buildings (this is an artists' world). Overall, this town just feels PLEASANT. There are palms, hibiscus, and bamboo everywhere. It feels like home.

Stroll through Le Cannet
http://mauiwriter.com/cannet

July 23

Mougins

Mougins is a clusterfuck of bad bus karma.[6] I miss two busses, get on one going the wrong way, have one pass me by while I'm sitting at the bus stop and I end up walking four to five miles instead, but it's worth the trip. Exceptional views sprawl the panorama, Mediterranean to the Alps, reminding me we are in the capital of Ahhhhh. This sweet villàge perché is filled with artists and galleries, restaurants and cafés, history and culture...and the MACM.

Take a peek here
http://www.mauiwriter.com/mougins

---

[6] But *"it's hard to stay mad when there's so much beauty in the world"*. American Beauty

◇

La Muséé Photographie mainly features photos of Picasso (the great), by his photographer friends, especially André Villers, whose donations to the city of Mougins made the museum possible. These virtuosos of the camera make Picasso come alive, both in his work and his family life.

Here it is:
http://www.mauiwriter.com/mouginsphotomuseum

◇

The pièce de resistance is the MACM, Musée d'Art Classique de Mougins, showcasing ancient Roman, Greek, and Egyptian art along with modern pieces in amazing juxtapositions. Four floors of paintings, sculptures, carvings (and more) puts Mougins on the map and visitors up close and personal with the beauty of the ancient world and its influence on neoclassical, modern, and contemporary art by artists like Picasso, Matisse, Chagall, Dufy, Cézanne, Rodin, Toulouse-Lautrec, Man Ray, Lichtenstein, Calder, Rubens, Klein, Degas, Dali, Warhol, and many others. Interactive touch screens further enrich the experience.

A mighty army of artists live here!
http://mauiwriter.com/mouginsMACM

26 Juillet

Jacked!

I'm off for a morning swim at the beach three blocks from my studio. It's a sensational day, about seventy-five degrees, and the beach is bare, except for a handful of souls. Drying off after a long swim, I'm reading F. Scott Fitzgerald's *Tender is the Night,* eBook version, set here along the Côte d'Azur.

Friends arrive by train at about eleven, and we're shopping along Rue Meynadier for about an hour when I reach into my purse to check something on my iPhone and...it's gone!!

I retrace my steps three shops back. I ask counter girls. I begin to panic. Sarah and Jake and I sit for lunch at a favorite bistro, and Jake texts my phone in French, offering a reward for its return. Nothing. Rien.

Running back to my studio, I mount the five floors, and get on my computer to change passwords, notify my banks and phone company, back up my laptop to another hard drive...just in case. I later go to the main police station, where I am reminded that the pickpockets in Cannes are "professionelle," that I'm not going to see my phone again, that the theives will strip the contents (contacts, photos, notes, identity, etc.), selling the data separately from the phone. The officer who assists me to complete a report on their most antiquated computer (with ancient software) just wants to go back to San Diego, where he was happier as a news photographer.

I spend the next few days having a pity party, feeling paranoid. I had done as recommended and taken photos of all my IDs, from passport and driver's license to birth certificate and travel documents. My press pass. My banking details.

Some stranger now has all of that.

And everything is lost to me.

By midweek, I'm processing my mourning. I visit La Poste to top up my French tele, switching to an unlimited plan. I'm lifting out of my funk and decide to take a bus up to Villa Domergue. A little afternoon jaunt. I am dropped off about half a mile below the Villa, so I hike. What a thrilling spot, with magnificent views of Cannes. Again, I wish I were rich and living in a different time, with gardens and leisure.

After a couple of hours there I begin walking downhill and, as with so many of my discoveries, I chance upon Chapelle Bellini, a storybook church, turned art gallery. I miss the 2 pm bus, so I walk all the way back to Cannes, another two miles, landing in an Arab section of town I've not seen before.

Deciding I need to visit the Apple store, again, I walk to the shop below the train station. The manager tells me the new iPhone 6 is coming soon, and I should wait. I leave without a smart phone, determined to live without one for awhile, at least while I'm out on the island. I buy a little notebook and a pen, flashlight, recharge my camera. I can write and shoot without my iPhone. What a concept.

4 Août

A fabulous day in St. Tropez

My friend, Laura, and I hop aboard the Trans Cote d'Azur in Cannes and cruise the scenic coastline of hillside villas, mountains, and fishing villages, arriving in just over an hour. It's the jet-setting town of fabulous fashion boutiques, expensive restaurants, yachties, artists, and celebrities. St. Tropez hosts nearly 6,000 residents and up to 100,000 tourists per day in peak season. Brigitte Bardot put this charming village (and the bikini) on the map in the 1950's, and today's stars keep it there.

Aside from great people-watching, St. Tropez is still a charming French port, discovered by artists, with cobbled back streets, markets, local shops (€5 panini, with choice of drink), and neighborhood parks, complete with games of boules and pétanque. But restaurants like Senequier (€9 un café) and hotels like Byblos (€3,000 per night) cater to the rich and famous in their own enchanted enclaves.

The collection at Le Musée de l'Annonciade, *"The color in the light of the East: from Delacroix to Matisse"*, features Signac, Cross, Bonnard, Derain, Vlaminck, Delaunay, Picasso, Kandinsky, and of course Delacroix and Matisse. It's an engaging and unusual collection, filled with the light the French Riviera is known for.

We drop by one of the beaches, then hike up to l'Église Notre Dame. As the day lengthens and yachts come and go, the sky morphs even bluer, if that's possible. On the boat trip back, we again zip by the famous Corniche D'Or, arriving in Cannes before six. Home sweet home.

Checkout the photos here,
and enjoy a day in St. Tropez
http://mauiwriter.com/sttropez

Magnificent Monaco!!

What can one say about this beautiful, fabulous, sparkling place? That it has EVERYTHING - glamour, a vielle ville, classic port, gorgeous structures and parks and gardens and views ...amazing views. Food...exceptional food. A subterranean train station with posted schedules and lifts that work, buses that run on time...and Ferraris and Lamborghinis - eye candy for the rest of us.

And art...did I mention the ART?!!

Take a peek here!
http://www.mauiwriter.com/monaco

Art Lovers

"Art Lovers", the current exhibit at the fabulous Grimaldi Forum in Monaco, is simply brilliant! Bellissimo!!

It's a labyrinth of fun and fabulous, disturbing and explosive art from the collection of François Pinault, who owns one of the largest collections of contemporary art worldwide. It represents thirty-three artists and forty major works by artists like Maurizio Cattelan, Jeff Koons, Takashi Murakami, Rudolf Stingel, Damien Hirst, Giulio Paolini, Yan Pei-Ming, Zhang Huan, Sturtevant, Charles Ray, Bertrand Lavier, Jonathan Monk, Sherrie Levine...the list goes on. Sculptures, paintings, mixed media, film. More.

The grand opening and icon for the show is Jeff Koons' Hanging Heart (Red/Gold, 1994-2006, high chromium stainless steel with transparent color coating)

The show is a pathway into the diversity of explicit or intimate dialogues carried on between works of art, and their reinterpretations by artists, past and contemporary. And YOU, the viewer.

This show *"... underlines the beautiful idea of the co-presence of several works in the heart of a single one, the fact that when one is in front of a work of art, it's not the only work one is looking at, but several, and perhaps all the works of art ever done. What it expresses most of all is the fact that this relationship between art works is placed, in the vision of the artist and especially in the vision of the viewer, under the sign of pleasure, of the game and of the love of art."*

Martin Bethenod (Curator).

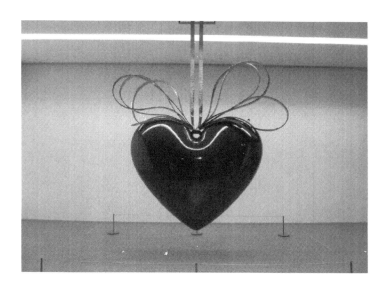

Don't miss it!
http://www.mauiwriter.com/artlovers

13 Aôut

Overcast, with a chance of tears

An overcast sky, like a bruise, subdues the market today, with many vendor stalls empty, others barely populated. I buy two bags full - a cantaloupe, two white nectarines and two bananas, swiss chard, carrots, lemons, cucumber, compte, saucisse de pays. The olive guy calls to me from across the expanse. I send him a "bon journée" back, making my way to a café for the €2 special - un café et croissant. And observing fellow beings.

M comes. I am loving our sweet, uncomplicated time together. He cooks, feeds me, helps me do laundry, hangs out til two in the afternoon, when we walk to the train station, and he heads back to Nice. I miss him immediately.

I turn on the news. Robin Williams takes his life. I watch clips, so sad, remembering how happy he always made me feel.

Little droplets descend from the grey, and the cafés that surround the market fill, shoppers taking shelter under large umbrellas, enjoying wine and conversation. I am home now as the rain comes, easy at first, then hard, like tears when you've lost a friend.

Frejus & Saint Raphael

The SNCF train (French National Railway) speeds by numerous beach towns, arriving inland at Fréjus, near the old town, filled with Roman ruins. But it's so French! Light peeks through, illuminating streets and squares. There are large squares with vendors and churches, tiny streets filled with cafés and artist's galleries, stones and shutters worn by centuries. It's an absolutely lovely day, about eighty. A true blue expanse of sky hovers, with an occasional billowy cloud dancing through like a nymph.

At Place Calvini, I duck into La Cave Blanche. It's so Parisian. Centrally-located in the old town, it could have been on a little street in Paris, with mottled light coming through the plane trees, bouncing off the adjacent cathedral wall, playing on textures of stone and brick.

The waiter teases me, "what is a beautiful woman like you doing alone?" Then Louis gives me first class service and a delicious yet inexpensive lunch of steak, frites, salade, and a superb vegetable flan...for only twelve Euros. A nice red (of course), and a panne cotta with apricot sauce. Afterwards I wander into the archeological museum to learn a little, then find a bus down to the port. I run into the championship Lyonnaise playoffs between Nice and Fréjus, teams of four serious sportsmen, playing their boules hearts out. I engage some fans in conversation. They're as serious about their boules as their football.

A long promenade hugs a mile of beach, leading to St. Raphael and its Basilique Notre Dame de la Victoire. I stroll and shoot, stop to enjoy a lemon gelato, eventually taking the TVC (high speed European trains) home. Again, there are no stops, just beach towns flying by.

Mathieu arrives at 9:30 for our best sex yet.

Enjoy Frejus ~ St. Raphael
www.mauiwriter.com/frejus

Stunned and altered again

I thought so much would change, untethered, homeless, but today - the same indecision, loneliness, paranoia...remnants of my PTSD. I clutch my bag (after being pick-pocketed), fear each step (following three bad falls). Counting, counting. Stuck as ever, indecisive about where to go, what to do.

I am not happy about it, but it is what it is, and if I am learning anything - through the stolen phone, broken promises, strange incidents - it's to let things be as they are. Including myself, with all my emotions or emotionless moments. What is it in me that expects happiness all or most of the time? that demands answers? Life is such a mystery, and despite a deep wanting to know, I do not. Embracing the mystery takes courage in these times, takes faith, and an unshakable knowing that this too will pass.

All of a sudden Mathieu is at my door...with dinner.

"...everyone in the world wants to be with someone else tonight, together in the dark, with the sweet warmth of a hip or a foot or a bare expanse of shoulder within reach. Those of us who have lost that, whatever our age, never lose the longing; just look at our faces. If it returns, we seize upon it avidly, stunned and altered again."
                                                                Roger Angel

Beautiful Cannes

I'm on the top floor of a five-story walk-up...a little studio in Le Suquet, Cannes' old town (vielle ville). From the open French windows, a get a constant sea breeze and scan over red-tiled rooftops to the port, the Film Festival Palace, the Croisette of Chanels and Guccis, and the curve of beach, setting Cannes off from the deep blue Mediterranean.

It has been my home now for seven weeks - a walk, bus, boat, or train to nearly everything I want to visit still. I add Paris to my wish list this morning. And Spain.

I break for an almond croissant, a pillowy confection from the patisserie on the corner, my first in France (stuck so on chocolate ones). "Oui, oui, bon bon," as my friend, Yvonne used to say. The last time I did any real time in France was with Yvonne, following a FIABCI (Fédération Internationale des Professions Immobilières or International Real Estate Federation) conference in Montreux (Switzerland). We rented a car in Geneva, heading south through northern and coastal Italy, along the Riviera, up through the Provence and through the chateau and wine regions into Paris. Ah, Paris. I think now about going again. Pourquoi pas? (Why not?)

I leave tomorrow for a week with the monks on isle St. Honorat, a 20-minute ferry from Cannes, returning at the end of the month to another sweet little apartment just two blocks away in Le Suquet, my home base for further exploration and discovery. Arles, Avignon, Aix en Provence, other little villages nearby are on my bucket list. I don't know about communications on the little island or when I'll be back in touch, so bon journée mes amis.

Enjoy these images of beautiful Cannes
http://mauiwriter.com/cannes2

Sanctuary

Abbaye Notre Dame de Lérins
l'île St. Honorat, France

The Island is stunning! It glistens in the Mediterranean, off the coast of Cannes and the Côte d'Azur in southern France. Vineyards sprawl through the interior, and seven chapels, numerous historical homes, fortresses, forests, turquoise water, and magnificent views hug the coastline. It's a natural preserve, with pheasants and sea birds, eucalyptus and pine, palms, wild blackberries, and the ever-present tower of the abbey.

Just a twenty-minute ferry from the mainland, it's only about four kilometers around its forty hectares, with a couple of crossroads - an easy walk for day trippers, who come to get their tranquil on, stop at the church for midday mass, pick up a book or a bottle (or other monk-made products) at the gift shop, and enjoy a gourmet lunch at La Tonnelle Restaurant. Perhaps a swim, before returning to busy lives. The last ferry departs at six pm, leaving behind twenty monks, forty retreatants, nine student volunteers. And silence.

This Lérins isle lies south of isle St. Marguerite, larger and famous for one of its prisoners, 'the man with the iron mask'. The fort now houses a museum of modern art, and both islands are under the city of Cannes. I am staying for a week (E300, including meals) to photograph the natural beauty of the island and interview monks and residents. And to get my tranquil on.

The Monastery is a spiritual resource. Room 12 is spare, tidy, monasterial, with a small bed, desk and chair, sink and shelves. A French Bible. An arched window looks over the courtyard, through the lemon trees to a vast sky, dotted with puffs and billows. There is a private prayer room, a library. Toilets and showers are at the end of the hallway, open by arches, looking down to a garden and a private pathway to the church, open day and night for retreatants, 9 to 6 for visitors. It's quiet except for the cicadas and the sea, which carry on a conversation, competing for my attention until chimes sound with the horn of the last ferry to the mainland.

Vespers is at 6:00. One by one monks, dressed in white robes with belted and hooded black tunics, enter, taking their seats in the chancel in the front. One greets us in the nave, eyes sparkling. A tenor begins to chant, his sound traveling up the piers to the vault's apex, filling the space...and me. The other monks and retreatants respond in antiphony. After ten minutes of this, six monks circle in the center and pray in four-part harmony. We respond. It is mesmerizing. I tone. Frère Etienne reads (his voice echoing) for about two or three minutes.

Between the echo and the French, I have no idea what he is saying/praying, but his voice is melodious and kind.

I love that they chant their prayers. The toning heals me, brings me back to some original innocence. Alternating responses and more chants are led by different monks in different parts of the church, the sound dancing through the space, mixing with centuries of song embedded in the stone, then embracing the congregation. Standing and sitting, bowing, listening. A prayer is read as twenty monks file out. Silence fills the space behind them.

A Paradise of prayer and brotherhood, isle St. Honorat is home for 16 centuries of war and peace to the monks of Lérins Abbey. It is first occupied by Caprais Honorat and a few companions between 400 and 410 AD. They form a community of monks, which grows rapidly in this (then) Roman province. A troubadour sings, hence we know the stories of Honorat, who becomes the Bishop of Arles later in his life. In the 5th century priests can marry, and the wives are kept on neighboring St. Marguerite isle. Benedictine vows are taken in the 7th century.

Over the years Italians and Spanish occupy the island, and in 734 all the monks are massacred. The island is later sacked by Genovese pirates. Monks are captured and enslaved in Spain. French royalty occupy for awhile in the 1700s, and the Abbey is closed during the revolution. Near the end of the 18th century it is nationalized and protected under the French.

Today twenty monks live and work here, ranging in age from 28 to 82, most between 50 and 60. A high of forty occupied the island in the 1980s, following a recruitment and revival by the young sisters who came during WWII (when the orphanage was closed) and lived here until 1991. Respecting the rule of St. Benedict based on prayer and work, the monks rise early for 4:30 vigil, then work and pray throughout the day, overseeing (with twenty paid employees) all the businesses of the island:

- Winemaking (also a distillery for Lérina and five other liqueurs)
- La Tonnelle Restaurant and retail shops (physical and online)
- Boat company - with a barge and two ferries, bringing 90,000 guests and goods to the island
- Guesthouse (runs at virtually 100% occupancy Easter to November) - 3,000 per annum
- Teen and volunteer programs, conventions, exhibits, special events

...all with no days off and only one week to ten days of vacation a year, usually taken mid November to mid December, when the island is closed to guests and visitors.

Vendange. It's harvest time, and retreatants and other volunteers work side by side with the monks, picking grapes. Known for their wine-making, the monks have won numerous awards with their Pinot Noir, Syrah, Mourvedre, Chardonnay, Clairette, and Viogner grapes, which excel on coveted terroir. Chardonnay and the reds are aged in oak. An exceptional extra virgin olive oil is pressed from the olives, whose groves mix with the vineyards.

I meet with winemaker, Frère Marie, for a tour of the winery. He reminds me that since the middle ages, wines were grown on only one and a half hectares and for local (monk) consumption only. In 1991 present day monks celebrated their first commercial bottling, and today they grow (without herbicides) on 8.5 hectares, producing 40,000 bottles of premium wines, 60% reds.

Frère Marie, a graduate of the viticulture school at Hyères, has been the winemaker for ten years. Alongside layman Daniel, the technologist and chemist, he does it all with only four employees and the other Cistercian monks. Marie explains that three things create the conditions here for great wine-making: climate (no winter), terroir (protection and isolation), and water (from one of two pure aquifers under the island). I personally think they add a bit of prayer.

When I first came to the island back in May, I tasted the St. Honorat 2010. It was the best red I'd had since arriving in France - cherries, earth, silence. I finished with St. Sauveur 2010.

Hallelujah, there IS a God!

It's an oasis of silence, where participants drop personal histories for introspection, inspiration, breathing...breathing. Where just to be is holy. *"When I find myself in times of trouble..."*, and aren't we all in troubled times? War, suffering, crises the world over. Here without the barrage of bad news 24/7, with no telephones (except a payphone on the path by the vineyard - *hello, God*), no internet (ok, for emergencies), no schedules other than those of the laudes, vespers, mass, and meals, we find a safe haven, a refuge. Pheasants know they will not be hunted. Retreatants know they will not be judged. No one is overworked. There is an ease of days, broken only by voluntary work and/or attendance at services and meals.

We break bread communally three times a day, six persons to a table, the meals taken in silence, starting and ending in prayer. Breakfast is self-serve: café, tea, or chocolate, toast and jam. Occasionally grapes are left in bowls on the tables from a picking. The main meal is midday - a salad of mixed greens or a caprèse, crunchy baguettes, fish or chicken (finished with a shallot and white wine sauce), dessert, coffee. Cheese and wine of course. It's a meal to look forward to. The evening meal is salad, croque or maybe a wild mushroom quiche, yogurt or fruits in season.

Silence stretches into the night, with the last

service ending at nine. I amble back to my room as stars load the sky. A jet, bound for Nice, flies through the big dipper. *Lucy in the sky...I* sleep in peace.

Pre-dawn I hike to the fort, and the sunrise takes my breath away! I circumnavigate the isle for two hushed hours, stillness broken only by the sounds of waves, trees having conversations with breezes, birds. After watching three teenage boys camping by the port, I complete my circle tour and sit in silence at the church, waiting eagerly for lunch. I fall in love with yet another island.

You can too
http://www.mauiwriter.com/sthonorat2

little island
oasis of brotherhood
and silence,
rest my body,
quiet my heart,
lead me to awareness
and the stillness
from which everything arises
      kj 25 Août, 2014

Sur la Rue, 4

Why did you come, and why do you stay here on this island?

Helene/Jean Marc Decitre Lyon & St. Etienne. Nurse, retired banker. 1st retreat, here 1 week.
"It's very beautiful here ...a savage beauty, wild and natural. Wild pheasants, creatures, the scents of flowers, the sea, lovely gardens, amazing architecture...calm, silence. Sun every day. We find friends here; the conviviality is very special, the solidarity with other retreatants, conference with the monks. Prayer. Plus des bonheurs. There's no telephone, tv, car, distractions. The mossies are a bother, but the oxygen is great. Breathing...breathing..."

Jean Pierre Villain. Near Paris. Retired educator. 4th time here, comes for a week each summer.
"Here I find harmony, harmony with time, with days. Segmenting makes the time pass in a way that feels timeless. I can go deeper. Nature brings a real-world time too: the sky, the sea, all of us connected. It's the unity of all things in harmony.

I live alone, so each retreat I get to commune with others, with the whole world. It is a freedom to have no separation. We give to each other in this life. We all rise. We pray, think, eat...together. Here I find harmony with myself and others. It's paradise. I hope it stays small. I love the life, the work (yesterday I picked grapes), the activity, the difficulties, the ritual of meditation, intellectual, physical work. There's freedom in this. Peace. The best reason to be with others. Bonheur." (happiness)

 *Jean Baptist Charentenay, Paris. 1st time here, here 4 days. Manages a very nice retail store for men's shoes "Here I feel the love of Jesus and can be patient in his love. I can be a brother to the brothers and the others. The place is magical - how good God is! To feel the generosity of God our Father, who gave us all of this, gives so much to the billions on this planet. To meet others in that place of humility and love, others who share our belief in God...to melt in the arms of God, staying close to his heart. I would love even more silence at this sanctuary, but to hear His voice, to hear his truth. Spiritus Sanctus."*

Father Andrew Wadsworth Sussex, England. 2nd retreat, staying 9 days. Invitation of frère Gianni, friend from Italy. Priest at St. Wilfred's Bognor Registry for eight years. Priest for 26 yrs.

"I come for the prayer, the silence, the rhythm of the prayer throughout the day. R&R is nice, but retreat is different from holiday. It's important for perspective, to put God back into our busy lives. I love the history of this place - St. Patrick (Ireland), St. Augustin (Kent). To do pilgrimage in a holy place is wonderful."

Laurence Le Deodic. 6th year, here 1 week. Sports educator from Gradignan, near Bordeaux.

"I work in a school, so I volunteer here in the office. The environment is magic! Everything here opens the senses, develops body and soul, spirit, the heart. I love the contact with the brothers and retreatants, the silence and the friendship. It's such a beautiful ambience...and to have church every day. The weather is perfect! So why don't we have a garden? I wish we had more fresh, healthy food. Freedom comes from our choices. Here one makes better choices. Peace."

Frere Colomban.
Monk, Lérins Abbaye.
Came here in 1990. Has been here since, except for 14 years at S'Enlenque Monastery, near Avignon.

"A friend told me about the island and abbey, and I first visited in 1985. It took me five years to leave my life as a teacher in Aix en Provence, husband and father, and make the choice to be here. I stay for the same reason I came: liturgy, community, work - the organization of daily life around service to God. Nature and this beautiful place. God is everywhere, but I think here we are a bit closer to Him. We are so spoiled here. We had better make the best of it."

Speaks great English. Plays Keith Jarrett. Blesses me.

Frère Gilles. Monk, Lérins Abbey, since 1973. Came as a noviate with 3 brothers and 3 sisters of Bethlehem back when sisters lived on the island too. Works mostly with the guesthouse and teaching theology to noviates.

"I stay by rational and providential choice. Because this monastery is a bridge of occidental and oriental monasticism of Cistercian monks, of which St. Honorat was the model, coming from Egypt, Greece, and Italy. We are a

brotherhood, a community. The life is prayer and work, and we are not closed, but open to the world."

Frère Marie. Monk 27 years, Lérins Abbey. Winemaker and Youth Development. Former electrician and pastor from Guillaume in the Alps, in the national park.

"Like most, I was called to a life of prayer and work here, to give my life to Christ. I found the monastic life because a Dominican Father told me about it here, and I thought engagement would be a challenge. I stay because it's my life. I would like to bring more young people to the pastoral life and to develop more agro-tourism here on the island."

2 Septembre

Food, Glorious Food

"Wine is sunlight held together by water." Galileo Galilei

It would be impossible not to do a chapter on something near and dear to every Frenchman's heart...food. Living here, where the food is local and luscious, it has grown near to mine as well. Not that I wasn't a foodie and a bit of a wine snob before. Having owned a restaurant and cooked for thousands, having raised a family and entertained both friends and business associates, I am pretty well-versed with regards to food and cuisine, but to be here is to know that some foods are simply better than others.

It's the quality of the food here that is remarkable. Whether it's a shallot or a chicken, there must be something in the growing of them to produce a taste so much more exquisite than back home. And with flavors this deeply satisfying, very little need be done to enhance them. A little olive oil, some fresh rosemary, heat. Time and time again I order a simple bucket of mussels, some opened in a light broth, some in a roquefort brine. Each time I am so happy to have chosen this simple food, with its delicate palate. With bread and a rosé, I'm complete.

Food offered, served, and eaten here is seasonal. Market tables sag under the weight of late summer tomatoes, berries of every kind. In spring asparagus are everywhere. Now zucchini and summer squash take its place. Fish and shellfish change week to week.

Then there is the perpetual baguette, that ultimate French food that appears on every table and under every arm. I shop around for months, finally picking two patisseries which I feel have the very best bread. I return often, buying half loaves since they don't keep. I have yet to have a bad croissant, while it is rare in the states to find a good one.

When I'm not going out for a meal and don't feel like cooking, I always have the perfect meal at hand - a simple baguette, some scrumptious cheese, and a nice wine. Perfect at my desk, on the beach, or sur le tren.

Grocery Haul, Cannes France

My new landlord meets the ferry back from the island, taking me to my wonderful apartment above the bistros at Rue Panisse. I settle in then go to Marché Forville and little shops on the square to stock up:

olive tapenade
2 cups fresh pesto
duck terrine
albacore tuna
1/2 doz. organic eggs
camembert (lg)
emmenthaler (1/2
  lb, sliced)
goat cheeses (2 sm)
crème fraîche
baguette
chicken sausages
veal loin
swiss chard (huge
  bunch)
lb. butter
mayo
apricot jam
penne pasta

red & sweet onions
garlic clove
shallots
arugula
watercress
bunch carrots
english cucumber
bananas
nectarine
apple
2 oranges
4 lemons
6 figs
almond croissant
  & café
Provence rosé
NY Times (weekend)
Nice-Matin (Sunday)

Total: €48.02

Beaches!

Anyone who knows me knows that I LOVE BEACHES! All beaches.

An old surfer, I am in awe of waves and sunlight, gliding through aqua, the bliss I feel embraced by Mother Ocean. It's pure magic! I've been going regularly while staying here along the French (and Italian) coasts - swimming, sunning, photographing, enjoying clouds and waves, watching people, my thoughts, the silence.

Very occasionally I go whole hog, renting a comfy lounge, with umbrella, service, and all the pampering a gal needs from time to time (E10-20 per day). It's better than therapy...and cheaper, with lunch and wine, than a round of mai-tais at Mauna Lani Beach Club. Here are my favorites:
Les Voiles in Nice (pictured)
Monterosso (Cinque Terre, Italy)
and La Croisette Beach Club here in Cannes

Onesies shout 'foreigner' here in France, so finally in early August I buy a bikini (on sale for E12) and go totally French. Back home this is a crime.

Liberté, Equalité, Fraternité...Vive la France!

New Bikini
Sun on my skin -
dancing, caressing -
where it hasn't been for thirty years
Wind on my skin -
tickling, teasing -
playing hide and seek with the sun
Water on my skin -
moving, stimulating -
reminding me of skinny dipping years
Sun, Wind, Water -
exposing me to sensations
and memories,
sweet, fleshed out

I'm at some beach or another for an hour or two almost every other day now, unless I'm out of town, exploring, or on assignment. A gentleman meets me at the shower one day at Midi Plage, says he was watching me swim. *"Vous nager comme un poisson,(you swim like a fish)"* he observes. We chat awhile in French before he leaves, and he is enchanted ("enchantée") to meet me. I return to my towel, under my striped umbrella (a gift from my landlord) and dive into my Saturday morning guilty pleasure, the Weekend International New York Times, cover to cover.

Now that it's September, European tourists are going, going, gone, and for the most part only foreigners and Ruskies are left. It means more room on beaches and streets, in shops and restaurants. And although water is much warmer than four months ago, I imagine that will change too with the days shortening. Yep, summer's over, but the beaches still beckon, warm and lovely.

Here are some of my local beach observations:

People-watching is the best on the planet.

About 40% of women are topless - young, old, all shapes and sizes - whether alone or with children or in couples...and not a fake boob in sight.

Men are 70% in speedos. Mostly the young wear shorts (and they're much shorter). Bulges everywhere

Seniors come earlier in the morning, families and couples later. Shallow and deep water aerobics for seniors @ 9 and 9:30 am

Beachgoers change from bikinis to thongs (or speedos to shorts)...under a towel, often assisted by friend or family member. And sometimes without towels.

Some lie on rocks when there's plenty of nice sand. Why?

The raft is full of kids on the weekend. Weekdays it's perfect for sunning alone.

On Saturday the shower is left on, not just 10-

seconds at a time as it is during the week.

The hawkers are all African, selling hats, beach gear, umbrellas, hair-braiding, Nice-Matin (best paper for practicing French and finding out what's happening along the Côte d'Azur).

Languages spoken: French, Italian, Russian, German, Scandinavian, Japanese, British, others.

Several white couples with a black child. A friend tells me adopting African children is popular.

Teenage girls still grease up with cocoa butter just like we used to.

Pigeons drop by, hoping for a few crumbs. One flies so close, his wings brush me. A first.

All sorts of ball games are played in the water - keep away, cross-over, football toss, netless volleyball...

Floating on the raft reminds me of Silver Lake...and the memories that come with various sensations.

Everyone in the world has an iPhone except moi!

A Muslim woman comes with her girlfriends, covered head to toe. They're all topless.

A woman in her eighties drags her portable oxygen tank & port, parks it, sets up her towel, gets comfy, takes off her bikini top, and lights up a cigarette.

Vive la France!

Some of the beaches I've enjoyed
http://mauiwriter.com/beaches

9 Septembre

Market Day

The market is the place to be. Marché Forville is the heart of Cannes cuisine, and every day is market day, except Monday when it's antiques day. It's peak growing season, and fruits and veggies are piled high on every surface from 7 am til 1. Fish, meats, and cheeses too, homemade pastas with a variety of sauces. The mushroom man's a regular, with his ten to twelve different varieties. Herbs and flowers spill into the aisles. Chefs and restaurateurs join mothers and couples, shopping for today's meals. There are little tables on the outskirts, where vendors offer '1 Euro' bags...or 'Gratuit' (free) produce.

I love the market - the smells, sights, colors, people! Walking two blocks from my apartment in Le Suquet, I make my way up and down all three block-long aisles, with full displays on both sides. I stop and chat with the vendors. They offer bites and samples: cantaloupe, nectarines, cheeses. By now I've developed a few favorite stalls, but I like to try a new one each time too. I've enjoyed markets all over France. They're my first choice for food, then the little boulangeries, boucheries, Casinos or Spars...or other small neighborhood markets, essential to life here.

"Bonjour, madame" comes at me. I smile back. I have been here long enough (and my French has improved enough) that almost no one mistakes me for a tourist anymore. My soul is being woven into a social fabric that holds this place, and all of us, together.

Cooking is a spiritual experience for me as I put some music on, dance a bit, then dig into cutting and prepping. I make a chicken curry: onions, shallots, garlic, carrots, potatoes, haricots vert, swiss chard, sage...all from the market this morning. It's glorious! Halfway through I invite a friend over for lunch. She brings the wine.

We eat well in France. The food simply tastes superior. It's fresh, mostly organic, and no GMOs. People here walk to the market, buy delicious, local foods, then carry a bag or two home for their meals. Since I have to walk my bags home, I choose carefully...and just enough for today and maybe tomorrow. Back home most drive to the market, buy a ton of food products from across the globe to stuff in their SUVs, then drive home. Doesn't seem very sustainable, does it?

I pick up some fresh spinach/ricotta pasta and about an inch of polenta, but then I need some roquefort. The cheese vendor is just across. I wander to the end of the marché to the patisserie for a still-warm baguette traditional, then sit with my Nice-Matin, un café et un pain chocolate. About twenty minutes pass when the aroma from next door floats by, so I stop in for half a chicken, fresh off the rotisserie. It's a difficult decision, with so many choices: roasting chickens, veal, lamb, ribs, pork loins.

People sit, enjoying their post-market break, discussing what they bought for diner. Shopping and eating are a big part of everyday life, the good life here in Cannes. La bonne vie. Lunches are still two-hour affairs over great food...and politics. But this morning I forget the politics of this country (and mine), lost in the sensuality of the market. People, borne of the rich earth and nurtured by mother sea, smile over their loaded tables or their café and croissant and infuse an overcast morning with a sunshine all their own.

I really need smell-a-vision to do this right,
but take a peek
http://www.mauiwriter.com/market

Yachting Festival, Cannes, France

Opening day at the Cannes Yacht Festival, highlight of the European boat show season, I grab my camera and head to the far end of the Quay St. Pierre for the first scheduled press conference at Serena Marine. It's hot, despite the sea breeze, but a chilled rosé helps. The new boat, Euphoria, is staged and gorgeous. This game is clearly a boys club (makers, shakers and press), with beautiful women strategically placed around for eye candy. Over 550 yachts and 50,000 visitors are expected here this week.

I meet three happy Italians (aren't they always the life of the party?) at the charging station, enjoying the refreshments too. Then we move on to Fairline Boats, which invites us to a large corner placement and serves up champagne and pupus. The Fairline Squadron 60 makes its World Première at this show, which sees more world launches than any other boating event. New CEO, Kevin Gaskell, introduces the new 48's and discusses the total reorganization of the company, including the replacement of twenty-two of its twenty-five managers. They're beginning to see market growth again and taking advance orders.

By seven I make my way up to the upper celebrity deck of the Festival Palace for the opening press party. I'm enjoying the views over the old port and Suquet as well as the Croisette, when I meet up with the press gals who processed my press pass the day before, and we mix and mingle. I've been noticing how multi-lingual Europeans are. Bien sur. Of course. The champagne is flowing, and I am the only one taking photos. Apparently the press do not cover themselves.

Midweek I take my friend Laura di Gianni for the mega yachts and a boat trip across to the other port (Canto) for more super yachts, 'used' yachts, and sailing ships. Helicopters and drones are hovering. Models are being photographed. Deals are being made.

Friday I visit the catamarans, staying for the big Sunreef cocktail party, with its gifts, fabulous live music, food and more champagne. Before heading home, I drop into the Sunseeker and Princess Yacht parties.

Initially I hesitated to go, this being a game for the 1%, but I learned a few things. Boats are also for families, charters & suppliers, small businesses; there's a growing demand for yachts that power themselves with renewables; there's big boat demand from Israel and the Middle East, and the Chinese market is growing fast; this is a people business. I watch the sea trials and deals being made on the boats. I love the people I meet, and I have to admit the yachts are amazing!

Take a look:
http://www.mauiwriter.com/yachtfest

Sur la Rue, 5

Adam - Fairline. Sydney.

"I've been with the company five months, after importing European boat brands to Australia for twelve years. I handle dealer visits and factories and shows to the Asia/Pacific region. I love this industry! It's a beautiful product, but mostly I love the people I sell to." He admits tough times since '08, but is excited about the current and projected future under new management. He loves having Kevin at the helm. *"He's the reason I came aboard."*

Christina from Poland at Sunreef. Former British Airways PR and Board Member.

"It's my first Cannes Yacht Festival as I'm new to the company, but I love it! This is a Polish company, founded in 2000. We have 80 two and three-hull yachts sailing all over the world, with most of our yachts for families from the Middle East, Israel, and the US. China is a growing market for us. They love our product, and whereas the British are all into the tech gear, the Chinese are only interested in the fun. We've customized one as a floating restaurant in Dubai. Actually they're all

customized, taking about a year and a half to build at our shipyard in Gdansk. Our 'Ché' model is our largest at 114 feet, with plenty of room for 8 guests and 5-6 crew. The'70 Power' has solar panels, wind and hydro power generation, LED lighting, and lots of power-generating and saving devices. It's a demand of the market. Our 165-foot 'Ultimate' will be our biggest yet. And we expect to enlarge our charter company as well."

Collin Sykes. Former CFO to midsize companies in the US and UK. CFO now one year with Fairline and happy with the progress which began with a deep listening to customers and dealers.

"2009-10 were dark years, but when banks retracted, investors started coming back in 2012; we took losses in 2013, with dealers overstocking. So we began financing our dealers, and today we have only shareholder debt, no bank debt on the balance sheet. The reorganization has turned things around with fresh ideas, new technologies."

Still cautious, he is moving forward with a waiting list.

"I'm feeling great loyalty to Fairline...trading up, helping others to build their careers up. I enjoy the hard work, hard-earned money, customers from the Middle East, Russia. Europe *is flat right now, but US is picking up. 2015 looks good, with new products and dealer inventory the lowest it's been in five years."*

Fairline's main competition is from Princess (LVMH Moët Hennessy • Louis Vuitton is a French multinational luxury goods conglomerate and Sunseeker (Chinese-owned).

Valeria Povergo,
St. Petersburg Russia. 27.
Director of Ordinar (new
online publication),
Former sub-atomic
 engineer.

"This is a prelude to the upcoming show in St. Petersburg. I'm staying a week here in Cannes and loving it. It's a great venue for the show...and kick-off for the season, with all of the brands, famous and unknowns alike. There are definitely unique brands here, which is my focus. Of course, because 'We're Independent and Interesting'. "

13 Septembre

A Weekend in Provence :
Arles. Les Baux. Avignon.

Arles. The train pulls out at 8:15 on a clear, radiant morning. I'm seated comfortably in 15/51, with the sea flashing by on the right, Alps on the left (yes, I'm sitting backwards). I surround myself in white light, safety, peace and joy...then all travelers as well. It's a little traveling mantra I've practiced for decades, mostly on planes. The temperature is perfect. The ride is smooth. With a transfer in Marseilles, I arrive at Arles by noon, and within minutes I'm lost. The Tourism Office is closed. (What? That's a first.) I find a pharmacie for directions. The Coliseum is "fermé" for a private event before the bull fights. An Arab guide sneaks me in with my press pass for "seulement un photo" (only one photo).

I make my way down through Le Jardin to find I have just missed the morning parade and fêtes, and the huge market is closing up as well. I take refuge in a church with a small art show, then I'm wandering (hot, tired, and hungry) until I find the bus stop, wanting now to just get out of dodge. After waiting about ten minutes, a woman tells me I need to go to the train station for bus 57. There is no way I can walk that far back, but a small shuttle bus comes and takes me there, free.

I arrive at la gare just as bus 57 leaves for Les Baux. Two women from Chicago and Kansas City strike up a conversation and are grateful for a translator. They're on a 10-day rush through London and France, and I'm exhausted just listening to them. The driver engages me, tells me I speak really good French. I hear that several times on this trip. It evokes a certain pride.

A few shots of Arles
http://mauiwriter.com/arles

Les Baux is a jewel, starting with the woman at the Tourism Office who issues all my press passes and prints out background info for the historic town and its best attractions. The hotel Le Reine Jeanne is just across the street, and my room is ready. I drop my backpack...and myself for a few moments, but I haven't eaten yet today, and I'm hungry. It's 3 pm, and the dining room is closed until 7, so I walk across the street to Au Porte Mages, where I spend an hour reviving. The restaurant is a haven of sun and shade, olive trees, and sweet service. Plat du jour is grilled lamb, with veggies and frites and a nice rosé. Afterwards I meander through town, making it up to the top and the Chateau, catch the film in the little historic church, then hike to the bulwarks and fortifications, walls and views, everywhere the bauxite.

I have a dinner reservation at 8:45, arrive promptly, and end up with a lovely warm fois gras over salad greens with sautéed apples et fruits rouge. Then I sleep sweetly for eight dream-filled hours.

Here's les Baux
http://mauiwriter.com/lesbaux

◇

Carrières de Lumières

I didn't know it before, but this show was my weekend's raison d'être. Uniquely fabulous, it puts one into the mind (and heart) of the artists And into some future world where art is alive in each of us.

The quarries were dug to extract bauxite and limestone, used to build the castle and the town of Les Baux. *Carrières de Lumières - Quarries of Lights* - is amazing enough, but the show, with its stunning images, displayed as never before, is incroyable!

"Klimt and Vienna - a century of gold and colors" showcases 100 years of Viennese painting, with a trip to the heart of the colorful, bright works of Austrian artist Gustav Klimt, his contemporaries, and those he inspired.

enjoy a slideshow here
http://www.klimt-vienne.com/klimt-et-vienne-un-siecle-dor-et-de-couleurs

Technical Specs:
Total Area of projections: 7,000 m^2

Height of projections: 6-14 meters
Running time: 35 minutes
Equipment: 100 projectors, 26 speakers ...
Number of projected pictures: 3,000

"This show is a work on emotion, to feel what the artist in question wanted to convey with his work. This is why music is so important; the goal is that all the senses are awakened to capture that emotion. My interest is to give the public the opportunity to see art differently."

Gianfranco Iannuzzi

Klimt show:
https://www.youtube.com/watch?v=XCNRYjStJ-g

Culturespaces is the producer of this magnificent show. It is explained thusly by Bruno Monnier, CEO:

"Our mission is to help public institutions to stage their heritage and develop their cultural and touristic attraction. It is also to democratize access to culture and for our children to discover our history and civilization in remarkable cultural sites."

Vive la France!

I enjoy a lovely light breakfast at Le Reine Jeanne, looking out from my little inn over the bauxite landscape, then check out. It's only €100 for the room, dinner, and breakfast.

Avignon. Catching the 11 am bus, I wind through little back roads with farmhouses, greenhouses, vineyards, orchards, olive groves. This must be the bread basket of France, Europe even. The bus driver navigates his Mercedes Benz and rocks some great American music from Van Morrison to Michael Jackson as we pass rivers and irrigation systems, fields of broccoli and cabbage, apricot orchards, cherries (still).

The villages each have a 'Credit Agricole' bank...and Roman ruins. It's a delightful hour-long trip. Entering the ancient Avignon wall, I'm just a couple of blocks to another extraordinary Tourism Office, where I'm issued press passes for the Pont d 'Avignon and the Palais des Papes. First the Pont, made famous by its memorable song:

Sur le pont
d'Avignon
l'on y danse
l'on y danse
Sur le pont
d'Avignon
l'on y danse
tout en ron

Climbing up to explore, I shoot several pictures of the bridge, its little church, the Rhone, and views. Then I dance...sur le pont.

After a walk back to the square, I enjoy a salmon grillé, too tired to deal with moules. Then I hop a little tourist train as a break from all the walking and shortly get to an overview of Avignon. The Palais des Papes is interesting enough, with its long history, art, and frescoes. It's gloriously gothic but claustrophobic and musty, so I don't linger. The seat of the Christian world in the 14th century, more recently recognized as a World Heritage site, it bears the mark of nine popes who ruled here until Rome took precedence.

Exhaustion overtakes me, and I plunk down at a small café on the main square for a Stella Artois, then call a taxi to shuttle me to the TVG train station, the new one, outside of town. It's clean and shiny, with good signage, shops, and restaurants. A trio peddle at a small bike stand to recharge their phones. Two young men share the free piano, riffing on a little jazz number that morphs into blues. It's a total bummer we don't do trains (and train stations) like the French.

I buy water and a sandwich for the trip home, which due to the TVG is just half the time of the trip up. We're off precisely at 20:40, passing by farms and factories (yes, the French still make things). I watch the sunset sprawl across a wide expanse of Provence, heading home. Cannes is the third stop, just two hours later.

Enjoy Avignon
http://mauiwriter.com/avignon

◇

Arriving home after 11 pm, I start to walk towards Rue Meynadier, but it's dark and there are shadowy figures in the doorways, and I am suddenly gripped with fear. First time since my arrival. Having learned the hard way not to ignore my gut, I turn and head back towards the station, spying two older women, arm in arm. I approach, asking if I can walk with them. The elder one moves back, afraid of me. "J'ai peur[7]," I admit. The daughter, links her other arm with me, and we all head down towards Rue Antibes, where late night cafés and lots of people help us feel safer.

Note to self: don't arrive late at night, alone. And if you do, remember Jim Carey's advice, " *Don't ever let fear turn you against your playful heart.*"

---

16 Septembre

Wanderlust

It's early on a Tuesday morning, so I boot up and tune in to my son. He's a DJ with Mana'o Radio on Maui, back in the islands, and his Monday night show comes on here in France at 5 am on Tuesday. I skype the station, "bonjour, mon petit fils. Ça va?" (Good morning, son, how are you?) After the first set, he shouts me out, sends aloha, tells his audience that his mom just called in from France. "Bunjur," he says, then he plays some Édith Piaf, Trenet's *La Mer*.

It's a bilateral world, and where I am here along the French Riviera is exactly twelve hours ahead of my ohana in Hawaii.

I am reminded of the many places I have been in the world. Over ninety islands and sixty countries. Still my bucket list is huge and my wanderlust always hungry. Like Charlie Chaplin, *"I'm a citizen of the world."* I feel it in my bones, never having felt a language barrier or a distance between myself and others in all my travels. Au contraire, the world over I feel a camaraderie; I feel a part of the great global family. It's heartwarming. And here in France I feel a part of something sweet, something cultured, elegant as a street scene or a masterpiece.

18 Septembre

3 French Vignettes :
Getting Around. Cote Cops. French Fashion.

Getting Around

I've been five months now without a car, and I love it! Transportation here is so good, I don't need one. Ok, twice up in the hill towns I would have appreciated wheels, but for the most part getting around is easy. A quick walk to the train station or the tram or to a bus and I'm whisked anywhere in southern France.

The options are clean, safe, and inexpensive. Men and young people offer seats to the elderly (et moi:-). Buses run here in Cannes until 3 am. Smart cars and bicycles can be rented by the hour or the day, from convenient locations all over Nice. Tourist trains and double-decker buses give a great overview of a new town, with hop-on/hop-off options for 24 to 48 hours, depending on the city.

Trains (both SNCF and TGVs) feature great views, as beaches and villages fly by while I recharge my camera battery, read my guide book or latest Nice-Matin. Almost all the train stations are undergoing improvements all the time. When was the last time you saw infrastructure getting improved in the states?

Train stations, old and new, have shops, cafés,

stationary bikes you can pedal while you charge your tech gear. And pianos, free for the playing. And someone's almost always playing - blues, jazz, classical. I arrive early one day at La Gare de Cannes for a trip up the coast to St. Rafael and Fréjus, check the schedule and platform, order 'un café' and sit to enjoy it with a warm, crispy chocolate croissant. I hear the keys tinkling faintly at first, then fill in the instrumental with the song in my head, *"when I find myself in times of trouble, Mother Mary comes to me, speaking words of wisdom, let it be..."* A young man plays Beatles tunes until my train arrives.

In Monaco a Lamborghini screeches to a halt to let me pass, then guns on. Walking, I have right of way at crosswalks. All over the Côte d'Azur roads are filled with bicyclists, like everyone's on a Tour de France. Or on a motorcycle. And for cars, digital signs throughout town show the available parking spaces in various garages. How thoughtful. Smart cars compete with Porches, and in Nice Auto Bleues are a great alternative - electric cars you can rent by the hour or by the day.

The French just move people around so much better than we do back home, where cars are a necessity. How I would love to hop a train from Ashland to San Francisco or Portland...or even Grants Pass. A coastal route would be divine. Like so many other things, I will miss the great transportation when I go back to the states.

Enjoy some images of the wonderful
transportation options:
http://mauiwriter.com/transport

◇

Côte Cops

I've been noticing and thinking about police, especially since the Ferguson killing saturated the media, with people here actually shocked that such a thing could happen. Living in the US, this is a regular occurrence, so as sad is it always is, it is not surprising. The French don't understand how our own police can kill with impunity (the killer hasn't even been charged), why there's no justice, or why Obama can't just go in and fix everything. Here the general public have no guns, and they're rare on police, so that kind of violence is virtually non-existent. Instead police work to serve and protect. On foot, bicycle, motorcycle, and horseback, they integrate themselves into communities, making all of us safer.

I ask them for directions, information, photos. I am not alone in turning to them instead of running from them. I watch as they stop people, engage them in gentle conversation, try to help, whether it's someone needing a shower (directed to the municipal showers) or a meal or assistance with their car or scooter. They're mostly on the street, not in offices until a call comes in. As pro-active peace-makers, they exhibit humanization (rather than militarization) of law enforcement.

There are so many things the French do so much better than we do - healthcare, food and product safety, recycling, environmental protection, education, transportation, consumer and community protection, etc, etc, etc.

See if you don't see a substance and style difference here:
http://mauiwriter.com/cops

◇

French Fashion
~ where a little dog or motorcycle helmet or baguettes under the arm are fashion accessories

Every time I'm in France, especially Paris, no matter how well I dress or how hard I try to look fashion-forward, I always feel like a country bumpkin. Not that I have any fashion sense back home, but here, oh la la - I'm in trouble.

A friend invites me to the Michael Kors fashion show, so I don the only dress I brought on the trip, the only shoes that aren't tennis shoes or flip flops, and join her for champagne, conversation, and fabulous fashion. We walk over a mile each way to the House of Kors, and I have such blisters on my feet the next day, I leave my cute heels outside my door for someone else.

There's something beyond fashion at work here - the shoes (spike heels even on cobblestones), the handbags, gorgeous shirts, skinny pants, the way a scarf is tied. It's about confidence, the tilt of the head, the excellent posture, tiny sizes.

Yes, people here are tiny. Young and old are smaller in general than Americans. In summer it's short shorts, bikinis, crop tops on younger women, linen pants, Italian shirts, and fabulous accessories on older ones. Now scarves and sweaters are tied luxuriously around necks and strappy sandals turn to kick ass boots. Men get in the act too. No mom jeans here, just hip-hugging, butt-flattering stretch jeans, scarves, shoulder bags...amazing shoes.

And why not? Just in Cannes there's shopping of every price and quality available. On the Croisette - Chanel, Gucci, Dolce & Gabana, Prada - high-end fashion houses, where a small handbag is €900, €1500 for a blouse. One block back, Antibes Street offers mid-range prêt-à-porter options, and back on Rue Meynadier bargains abound in local French and Italian clothing/shoe/accessory choices. A cute dress for €15, a blouse for €9, a €12 bikini.

Then there's the Suquet Street Sale, where locals turn out for the biggest garage sale ever. Blocks are filled with tables, ladened with fashion, art, antiques, everyday household items, and so much more. I buy a beautiful blouse and a pair of brand new swim goggles for €1 each.

In a town like Cannes shopping is fun and truly therapeutic. I buy an Italian blouse, a summer dress, leggings, sandals, and a bikini, and already I feel more French. Now if only I were a size 2.

French fashion show here
http://mauiwriter.com/fashion

21 Septembre

Dejeuner avec un amis

Pablo comes down from Germany for one of his regular forays into southern France. I haven't seen him since Maui, but we're old friends so it's an easy reunion.

He takes me to his favorite restaurant, Atoux & Brun, where we begin with a bit of Pastis, some olives, a baguette. Two dozen assorted oysters arrive on an iced platter the size of a football field. A Sancerre is opened, and we dig into conversation and oysters for a good hour.

He tells me he is moving down to the coast, and I am jealous. Loving the French lifestyle so, how I wish I could live here. I'm not alone.

The next day he insists on a little trip inland to the foothills of the Alps, past the villages of Valbonne, Opio, Gourdon, Coursegoules. The views from the switchback roads are stunning, now familiar, looking down onto the Côte d'Azur I've come to love.

In Coursegoules we stop in for a fabulous French

country lunch then walk it off around the vielle ville, shooting from every angle. The setting sun lingers just long enough to paint the drive down to Cannes in broad impressionist strokes.

25 Septembre

Firsts

I drop by Planet Sushi on the way home, remembering how great my last meal there was. This one isn't. It gets me thinking that seconds are usually never as good as firsts.

Remember your first dog? Your first A? First house? First love?

My niece posts that when she loves something, she wants more of the same. But is it ever the same?

A friend takes me to Super Viande, a new restaurant just off Marché Forville, and we enjoy the best hamburger I've ever experienced - a gigantic half pound of wagyu beef, cooked rare and to perfection, served on a buttery brioche. We go again in a few weeks. It is raw, completely different, disappointing. Laura gets sick.

I remember a night thirty years ago. A party at a friend's. A man who came home with me for a night of sweet love-making. I never heard from him again, but a year or so later I run into him. I ask "why?" I believe his answer, "I just couldn't. It had been such a perfect night, I didn't want to ruin it by chancing a second time."

I remember many firsts - how sweet they were. How powerful. My first arrival in Hawaii, gardenias and night blooming jasmine filling the air. My first sunset at Hapuna Beach - a mango pink horizon, punctuated by a green flash. My first time rounding the island on Rarotonga's little road. Remembering that turquoise lagoon with its powder beach still makes me smile.

There is something in us that wants double the pleasure of first moments, but can we really relive the magic of firsts? And is that why I am continually on a search for first moments, virgin experiences? New adventures?

Right now the sunshine lights the wall outside my window, throws shadows in patterns from the tree, turning in its season as I write. The flowers I bought yesterday at the market bloom in their unique pinkness. They will be different tomorrow.

Maybe noticing more deeply will help to re-create a first. Or maintain the aliveness of firsts.

My first published book began, after a week of writing, to write itself. I want another first like that. Another book that shares my passion, unwinds a bit of mystery...through me. I begin.

7 Octobre

Quick trip to Marseilles

An American friend has lost her passport, so she picks me up, and we drive down the coast to Marseilles, France's fourth largest city. It has a bad rap. And rep. I'm not quite sure why. Some say there are too many illegal immigrants. For some it's the crime. My experience, beyond the fashion, food, and beautiful harbor, was a sort of uneasiness. A little je ne sais quoi.

It only takes her about two hours, while I investigate the large square by the American Embassy at Boulevard Paul Peytral. Afterwards we walk to the port for moules with gorgonzola et frites. And the worst service ever. I would have loved to stay longer, but Cynthia has to work in the afternoon, so we cruise up to the highway and speed home.

12 Octobre

Théole et Napoule

I take the 20 bus to Coubertin where I wait over an hour for the 22 up the coast, arriving by 13:30 at Théole Marie, a charming little French beach town. Wandering around the square towards the seafront, I drop in at an exhibit of local artists, then settle at Palazzo Beach for a seafood risotto, sauvignon blanc, and wonderful café gourmand. I just recently discovered these little sweet treats - usually 3-5 small samples of the house desserts. What's better than a bite or two of apricot tarte, panna cotta with berries, chocolate mousse? And of course the obligatory espresso.

Onward to beautiful Mandelieu-la-Napoule and the Chateau de La Napoule, with its incredible story (and art) of Henri and Marie Clews. It's too late for the guided tour, but I'm allowed to meander through the castle and its extensive gardens au bord de la mer. A product of the Belle Epoch and the Clews, this restored chateau today is a national treasure, offering classes, exhibits, scholarships, soirées, and more...to support the arts and artists.

I realize on the bus home how much I love little beach towns. Especially ones with culture.

Take a peek
http://www.mauiwriter.com/theolenapoule

20 Octobre

Going Local sur la Cote

I've totally gone local - market and café in the morning, meeting friends later in the day, getting plenty of beach therapy, chasing live music. Writing of course. And taking my camera everywhere. I catch a Regatta at Plage Midi one day while swimming and sunning. Later I finally hop on the petit tren for an hour trip around beautiful Cannes, glad I discovered it before this little tourist trip, but happy to re-visit the beautiful sites and carry on a long conversation with the engineer, now that I can speak better.

I share a great day on isle St. Marguerite with Jake and Sarah (from Villefranche) and his family, visiting from the states. It's a boat trip to the island, a hike across, and a fundraiser swim meet. Jake represents the USA in the swim competition, and we all share food and wine after the trophies.

Cynthia and Mickey and I enjoy a fun day shopping at Cap 3000 in Nice. It's my first shopping center in France. And it rocks!

Laura and I go for a Piscine of champagne at the elegant Carlton. 'Piscine' means swimming pool in English. A piscine of champagne is a large glass of iced champagne. The service is impeccable, watching the rich and famous - good fun, and the champagne is literally ice cold.

Several of us end up last night at La Cava with plenty of wine, music, dancing. Live music and a lively crowd. Last Saturday Laura and I took the train to Antibes then walked to La Voute to catch my friend Pierre Bertrand, for jazz, good food, and company. The cafe gourmand is the best ever - petit desserts of crème brûlée, panna cotta with cherries, ice cream with chocolate sauce, tiramisu. We make the mistake of missing the last train, then the last bus home. Finally Laura calls her driver to pick us up for the trip back to Cannes.

When I get home, Rue du Suquet is still happening with late diners and street music. I watch the Pacific Express café from my window then shutter up and tuck in for sweet dreams.

Two of my other favorites are Maitre Renard, featuring a piano/female singer duo, playing French and American chansons and The Cotton Club, for late night rock, jazz, and dance music.

Let's talk about a little food porn. When my friends come from Nice one evening, they ask me to pick a great place for lobster and seafood. Asking around, Le Saint Antoine at the bottom of my street comes up, hands down. It's even recommended by other competing restaurateurs. So I make a reservation, the train arrives, and we all sit down at nine. Service is attentive but not intrusive, and the food is perfect. Mounds of lobsters, crab, prawns and shrimp, mussels, clams, and other shellfish eventually disappear, over champagne and great conversation. A few hours later we all agree it is one of the best meals of our lives.

Wandering along 'restaurant row', at Rue Hoche and H. Vagliano, following a long walk up and back from yet another museum, I pop into Panini Federale. The sandwich sign says, "Vini & Panini," and that's just what I get - a delicious

Italian red and a lovely panini of turkey, mozzarella, roasted red peppers, and arugula (roquette, as it's known here). Nicolas serves it all up with panache, some conversation, and a cappuccino.

It's surprising how many little restaurants there are in French towns. Every day it seems I discover another one, better than the last. So if you think the markets are wonderful and cooking at home is the best, don't worry, dining out options are endless, delicious, and for the most part very well-priced.

◇

I'm thinking about Ben Bradley today and how journalism used to be journalism, so I re-watch *All the President's Men* on Amazon. [Netflix is not yet available here.] Robards plays a great Bradley, and Redford and Hoffman are peaking in their respective careers. The story is as thoroughly engaging (without any car chases or killing) as when I first watched it, but the bugging, surveillance, and dirty tricks are far more pervasive forty years later. Ask Snowden. Assange. Follow the Money...

"A writer is a world, trapped in a person."
Victor Hugo

25 Octobre

Adieu, Cannes

This week I catch a beach day. The days are shortening. Trees color. The sea cools. I spend more time just observing the little boats in the port, the vendors at the market, the residents, now that the tourists are gone. I spend a quiet afternoon prepping the next two weeks of my trip, deciding I need more Italy, so I book Rome and Florence. Then London, where I'll spend two days with family before flying home.

It's finally my last day here in beautiful Cannes. I head to the pharmacie as soon as I can move I've been up all night in pain, the back thing, aggravated by carrying a huge box up to the poste yesterday. The pills from home don't touch it. The pharmacist gives me Voltaren, and by the time I finish the New York Times et un café, I'm good. Vive la France!

I go back to pack and clean my apartment, grateful for this sweet home base the last several weeks. I lunch at the Salsamentaria, sun pouring over my shoulders. Brando brings me a lambrusco. I have two more free cards and will leave them with my darling landlord. Brando was the one I met the first time here when they had just opened and I had just arrived...was that July? I tell him I'm off to Rome. We practice Italian (buongiorno, buonanotte, tutti bene), and he recommends the pork cheeks with fried polenta (guancialini di maiale al lambrusco con polenta fritta). OMG, best meal here yet! I may have to postpone veganism til my next life :-) I finish with un café and that fab little chocolate cookie they serve with.

It's been such a happy time here, and Cannes has far outlived my expectations. I'm feeling so grateful to have lived here long enough to taste the sweet experience of living in France. I'm off to Rome in a couple of hours. I'll bid adieu to Yvan, settle my account.

When we meet, he insists on taking me to the Nice airport. I cancel my taxi, and we have a sweet conversation along the way. He parks and takes me in, checking the schedule then buying me one last café, while we linger.

I will miss heading off around 8:30 to the market, browsing through the stalls, spying some tangerines along with a couple of apricots, some raspberries. A quick shot at the pharmacie to get a few things I can't back home without a doctor visit. I'll miss running into friends at the top of my stairs for kisses and news. I'll miss stimulating swims in the Mediterranean. Et ma petite affaire d'été. I will miss the French lifestyle and this loveliest of coasts. But I will take the joie de vivre with me.

Bid a fond adieu to Cannes
and the extraordinary Côte d'Azur
http://www.mauiwriter.com/cannes3

"The time passed extremely slowly, as time should pass,
with the days lingering and long,
spacious and free as the summers of childhood."
Edward Abbey

25 to 30 Octobre

Rome

As it turns out Yvan takes me to Nice Airport, parks and helps me in, buys me un café and waits until I'm able to check my bag and do security (so much easier than back in the states). Easyjet is efficient, friendly, and cheap by half the price. In an hour twenty I land in Rome, walk right through (coming from Europe) without customs or immigration and catch a E40 cab to my hotel, where, despite an online booking and several emails to the manager, I have NO reservation. It's after 11 pm, I'm hungry and tired and now a little cranky. The night clerk puts me in the only room they have empty and promises that Damiano will fix everything in the morning.

I'm in a little monk's room with a tiny bed, tiny space, tiny shower, no view, all the things I'd been specific about in my email requests. I haven't eaten all day, and they have no food. Still I sleep.

I've decided to take a quick trip back to Italy - for the pasta...and so much more. I have four days each in Rome and Florence. Words can't begin to describe this huge city of 3.5 million. It's sprawling, confusing, chaotic, disorganizing, dirty, frustrating. It's also scenic, historic, beautiful, delicious, and thoroughly enjoyable. I'm at a point where I can't keep up with the pace of my life, so here, unedited, are journals and photos from amazing Rome, Italy.

26 Octobre

By morning I'm looking for a room (my booking lost here), down the street and around the corner to another hotel. I look at the room. It is depressing, with NO wifi. I cross the street where Gigi at the Hotel Borromeo actually offers to help me out, opens his little address book, and starts calling around, finally finding me a cheaper room in a 4-star, right near **Via Veneto** (La Dolce Vita). A cab drops me at the entrance, and I enter a better world, where cherubs dance on the ceilings, and class is written all over. Michele books me right in, I drop everything in the room and head out into my first day in bella Roma.

After passing the American Embassy (grand, former palace of Queen Margherita, built in

1886), I get down to the metro, which the concierge has instructed me to take to the **Vatican**. I stop to negotiate a taxi driver for the day. He wants E200 for 4 hours! Instead I wait twenty minutes for the hop on - hop off bus, meeting a couple of women from Israel, here on a little spa holiday while doing some workshops. Then I hang with some wonderful Italians from Firenze, finally loading into the last seat on the double-decker (cold and windy), winding my way around Rome, gawking and burning through my camera battery faster than ever. I will return to the Colosseum and Piazza Venetia.

I hop off at the Vatican, too late for the Pope, but not too late for a pass at the National Museum, housed in the former cloister (town) of the popes and bishops in the 6th Century, **Castel Sant Angelo**. From the top, it has panoramic views of Rome. Walking through the little streets and squares, I get a real feel for how they lived back then. They lived like kings.

I wander into the little tourist office (the French do this so much better) past street performers and little shops to **St. Peter's Square**. It is HUGE, with thousands of people cuing up. Instead I ask a tour operator to recommend a nice restaurant, and he takes me around the corner to Satiricus, where Roberto makes an otherwise good lunch fabulous. He is attentive, fun, and incredibly efficient, handling dozens of tables with panache. When I ask if he speaks French or English, he speaks flawlessly in both then says he learned so many languages by working in the restaurant from age 13. He loves his work, and it shows.

I enjoy the piatto del giorno (plate of the day), tomato/basil salad with a huge buratta, arugula, nice balsamico. There's bruschetta, a carafe of nice red, sparkling water bottle, a delicious pasta carbonara, divine panna cotta, and Italian espresso. After no dinner the night before and nothing but coffee all day, it's perfetto.

After a very long walk home, the internet in the room isn't working, so I take my laptop down to the bar where Mauro pours a little amaretto in my caffé. I hang for an hour or so, catching up.

27 Octobre
After a great in-hotel breakfast, I walk downhill via different side streets, coming around the back of the palatial **US Embassy**, secured by the Italian Army, Italian and Rome Police, and local Security. At the bus stop I meet two Brazilian gals and we observe a whole street of smart cars, plugged in. I hop off at the fabulous **Stazione Ferroviaria**, where I take a ticket then cue up for forty-five minutes to buy my Thursday train ticket to Florence, enjoying a superb cappuccino and prowling through two floors of books at Borri Books International Bookstore. There are restaurants, a Nike store, Armani, others.

All set, I head downstairs to the Metro, spend €1.50 for a ticket and hop off in two stops at the

Coliseum. Built in 80 AD to hold 50,000 seats for its spectacular games, today it's Italy's largest tourist attraction, drawing over five million visitors per year. It's colossal. Bigger than imagined. Thousands of visitors are lost in it. Here history slaps you in the face then runs away with your imagination. It takes me about two hours - one to stand in the line for tickets (hey, it's Italy), one to enjoy this wonder.

Enjoy the Coliseum
http://www.mauiwriter.com/colosseum

I shoot the exterior and the arch, wander a bit, then decide to head towards **Piazza Venezia**, but I spy a bike, and Rome (yep, his mom named him after her favorite city) pedals me over, dropping me at a streetside ristorante on the plaza for a table in the sun, ravioli, a nice red, and a much-needed break. Completely satisfied,

I pace the piazza, heading to **Altare Della Patria** at the far end.

It's breathtaking, from the stunning memorial that anchors the piazza to the domed and roman buildings all around, from the buses that land and depart (making this the heart of Rome), to the pizza and pasta spots and lovely cafes, Piazza Venezia rocks! Walk your camera past the park and up on the very top of the memorial, via elevator. You'll be rewarded by monumental sculptures, stunning interiors, a film museum, and the most fabulous panorama of Rome.

Piazza Venezia
http://mauiwriter.com/pv

It's a long walk to **Trevi Fountain**, which is crazy with tourists and under construction, with most of it closed off for repairs. I grab a gelato then get a E6 taxi home - whew. I must have walked 8 to 10 miles today and hundreds of steps. It feels good to be 'home', editing photos and enjoying a nice Montepulciano after this rich, full day.

28 Octobre
Hiking downhill under overcast skies to Vila Medici, I find it's not open for a couple of hours, with an English-speaking tour (gratis per la stampa - free for the press) at noon. I carefully descend the 136 **Spanish Steps**, have a little conversation with a lovely Italian policewoman, brief negotiations with the horse and buggy

driver, then hop on   the Metro to **Piazza del Popolo**.

http://mauiwriter.com/pdp

The huge square hangs out in the sunshine. I tip the guitar soloist, playing haunting tunes while I photograph little street scenes all around the piazza. The **Leonardo da Vinci Museum** calls, but I don't have enough time today.

I put myself in a Fellini film by dropping by **Caffé Canova** on the town side of the piazza. The cappuccino is creamy and delicious. It's pricey, but hey, it's a celebrity. I engage my waiter, Angelo, who's been at the cafe twenty-five years and used to serve Federico Fellini. Friends of the film maker owned the café, so he hung out here every day with his friends, getting movie ideas, writing scenes, and drinking his favorite beverage, fresh-squeezed mandarin juice.

On the walk back, I sign a petition for Lautari and his program for les enfants. The Anglican Church has Vivaldi's Four Seasons concert tomorrow night. I calendar it.

The English tour starts as soon as I get back to the 1576 **Vila Medici**.

http://www.mauiwriter.com/medici

It's an extraordinary Renaissance Villa with stunning views of Rome, and our guide Luca is speaks English with a French accent. The French

Ministry of Culture & Communication handles this treasure acquired by Napoleon in 1803. He installed the French Academy here. Today they provide an artists in residence program (eighteen to twenty-four French and others) that piques my interest, and the details fire up my imagination about the Medicis, the powerful and rowdy popes, married for power and loaded with scandal - porno art, four hundred residents and forty prostitutes, tons of legitimate and illegitimate children, sinful messages in the commissioned art. These were lascivious times, not exactly all virgin Mary and sweet baby Jesus. Fascinated, I think of doing a book about the Medicis. I'd read it.

In the caffé, I order a jambon panini and red for the view over Rome and am joined by Parisian, Nicola, here as an intern at the Palace. We have a great conversation in French and English, then he buys me a caffé, and we linger over conversation about art and travel. And the Medicis of course.

Another one hundred thirty-six steps down (there's a huge crowd now) the Spanish Steps, and I'm not far to **Barberini Palazzo**.

http://mauiwriter.com/Barberini

...just past the Spanish Embassy, half a mile down the shopping street, around the piazza, and up the hill. Caravaggio's Man with a Lute takes the first exhibit, then I stroll through the neglected gardens of the palazzo before entering the palace for the regular exhibit. It is gratuit and good thing, since a whole floor is closed today due to a shortage of personnel, despite there being two in every room on the other floors. Amazing Art: Caravaggios, Raphaels, Garofalos, Berninis, Tintorettos, El Grecos, Renaissance, Roman, and Venetian.

A quick taxi uphill (just can't walk any more), a vodka tonic at the hotel bar (Mauro translating for the bartender), and up to my room to download and edit and write...

And sleep.

29 Octobre
All out, full tilt today, I take the Spanish Steps labyrinth underground to the Metro to the **Vatican**, where street hawker, Eslam, negotiates me into the Maya Tours office just as Jad is heading out with his group. I jump on and am glad I did from the moment I spot the enormous lines. Waiting another hour or two just isn't in my plans today.

A rare Syrian Christian, Jad Butri is the only Arabic guide at the Vatican. His family is under the protection of Assad, and he came in 2010 under diplomatic coverage to Florence to get his PhD in archeology. His thesis is about the old monasteries being destroyed in Syria.

We first visit the gardens, inside and out, then

the museums of Renaissance art, sculptures, Raphael rooms, and the famed **Sistine Chapel**, jewel of the Vatican, where young 31-year old Michelangelo initially refuses the job because he is a sculptor, not a painter. But one doesn't refuse popes, so after working three weeks with painters and studying bodies from tombs, he tells them to leave, working alone and finishing this masterpiece four years later in 1512. At 61 he paints the Last Judgment, and a month after he dies, one of his students covers up the naked bodies for the new pope. The 1979-99 restoration is financed by Japan.

Jad leaves us in the Chapel, and we continue on ourselves to **The Basilica**, built by a brain trust of Renaissance architects and capped with Michelangelo's dome. Inside, an enormous space is filled with priceless jewels, artworks, and the famous Pièta. The Basilica is Italy's 'largest, richest, and most spectacular church', protected by 150 Swiss guards, who live here with 550 clergy.

The Vatican Museum
http://mauiwriter.com/vatican

and the Basilica
http://mauiwriter.com/basilica

Exhausted, I stop in Ai Fienaroli near my hotel for a lovely late lunch of fresh ravioli, stuffed with chestnut purée, buratta, and black truffles with a porcini mushroom sauce and a nice

Sangiovese. The flavors are delicate, unique, seasonal and sensational. I could write poems about this food. I've learned to let the waiter guide my decisions, so when Simoné insists I try the ricotta mousse with pistachios and chocolate along with my caffé, I do as I'm told. Ridiculously delicioso! I'm on a food high. I want to linger, watching the lively families, couples, and business associates at this local spot. Just when I'm thinking an afternoon affair would be perfetto, he brings a chilled limoncello instead.

I planned the best for last, so I stroll through the park, filled with electric carts, bicycles, segways, scooters, children, elders, and lovers, to the **Borghese Palace**.

http://mauiwriter.com/borghese

It's stuffed with important art masters and has NO lines. They keep the crowds to a minimum by limiting entrance, which requires reservations days in advance, and mine's from 5 to 7 pm.

After dark when I leave, just three blocks from my hotel, I take a few wrong turns and get lost, arriving back (finally) 30 minutes later. I'm missing my gps and flashlight on my long-gone iPhone.

Rome is exhausting and exhilarating...
here's one last peek:
http://mauiwriter.com/rome

30 Octobre to 3 Novembre

Fabulous Florence

Florence - sheer beauty, ravishing, sensuous, glorious. Oh, how I love this city!

30 Octobre
Travel day. I find a bit of apprehension every day I'm doing major travel - the things left behind, five warnings in fewer moments at stations, to watch out for pick-pocketers, people offering to help with your luggage, etc. But that's another worry - the luggage. I've done six months now with one small suitcase and a backpack. Still when I'm hauling them, it's a 2-Voltaren, hot bath, wish-I-had-a-masseuse day.

The fast train to Florence is quick and easy, with free coffee and snacks, wireless, chargers...and sprawling views of the Italian countryside, where vineyards and solar farms cover the floor, beneath hill town castles and forts. A quick taxi to my hotel on **Piazza Santo Spirito** lands me on the top floor in a room made for a princess.

I arrive midday at **Palazzo Guadagni**,

http://mauiwriter.com/PalazzoGuadagni

where Olivia (Italian) and Atish (Mauritian) show me around to various lounges, a wrap-around terrace, library, dining room, finally vaulting to the top floor where I walk through my personal library into a lovely, light-filled room. It's spacious, with beautiful wall art and a bathroom (and finally a bath) bigger than my last apartment. Within minutes I'm sprawled on my king bed, wireless working, looking out over Florence. It's spectacular!

After a few hours orienting myself to Florence,
Piazza Signoria
http://mauiwriter.com/ps

and the **Piti Palace**,
http://mauiwriter.com/pitti

I take dinner at a nearby trattoria, where I meet a honeymooning couple from San Francisco and enjoy pasta with squid ink and porcini mushrooms in a spicy Tuscan sauce. The dark chocolate soufflé cake with a runny white chocolate and blue cheese center is divine. Move over Roy's.

31 Octobre

Heading out into the day, I cross two bridges down from **Pont Vecchio**, winding through back streets to **The Tower of Palazzo Vecchio**, where I climb 250 steps from the 112 already up. The views are significant but mostly blocked with ropes, and there's another guard on his smart phone. I enjoy a little of the museum, note the graduation ceremonies downstairs, and soon am out into the Piazza Signoria, wandering past a carousel and small shops on my way to the **Duomo**.

http://mauiwriter.com/duomo

Even looking down and seeing its enormity from the Tower, it's hard to fathom once I'm here.

Afterward circumnavigating inside and out, I duck in a little side street where the sign outside Sasso di Dante reads, "life is too short for cheap wine." It calls my name. Soon I'm enjoying a beautiful Chianti and gnudi fiorentine ricotta & spinaci al burro salvia e parmigiano. (ricotta/spinach balls in sage butter with parmesan shavings). Mouth-melting. The waitress explains the cover (coperto - table set up fee). There no water, the police have denied their permit to serve tap. I miss the free, cold carafes of delicious tap water in France, as well as no cover charge.

Shooting street art on the way back from Bardello, which is closed, I drop into **St. Mark's**, where I notice a sign for 'Opera tonight' - Love Songs...and step inside, where I catch two musicians practicing. He's on piano and singing baritone. She fills the space with a voice made for Carmen. It' a thirty-minute treat.

Back in my princess' room I edit photos, write a bit, putter about the hotel, then go to Ricci's on the piazza for a meal of pappardelle and wild boar. I shoot the Halloween kids around the fountain, then head up for a good movie in my room. Buonanotte, Florence.

1 Novembre
I sleep like someone enjoying death, waking to shower, email, facebook, blog, then breakfast in a room filled with prisms, little sparkly rainbows dancing around the room. Atish makes a seriously delicious espresso, and the croissant is stuffed with an almond cream.

Some of the charms of a great city are all the little street scenes - the chess shop, window art, little markets, musicians playing for coin. While shooting great art all day, on my way to the original David (not the one on Piazza Signoria), I cross the Arno and come upon a musician who plays hauntingly beautiful sounds so unique I stop for a long listen, tip generously, then walk about for miles, enjoying the streets of Florence.

Enjoy the streets of Florence:
http://mauiwriter.com/street

Attempting to follow my directions to the **Accademia Gallery** - *Walk thru St. Spirito Piazza to Pont S. Triniti, via Del Tornabuoni, past Piazza Palazzo, right on Dela Rebublica, left of Calinala...Borgo san Lorenzo/P. Medici, right Via Cavour, right Via Degli* - I get lost, but the wandering in Florence is so good. I amble into an Italian food show, then drop by a *"Picasso & Spanish Modernity"* exhibit at **Palazzo Strozzi**. The event covers from 1910 to 1963 and features Miro, Dali, Gris, Gonzales, Tapies, and others, along with Picasso.

Eventually I arrive at the Accademia, pay E4 to skip the long line (€20 without a press pass). Michelangelo's original **David** is the main draw, and it's spectacular!

It makes the excellent copy on Piazza Signoria, well...look like a copy. I trip on the sculpture rooms, the Florentine art, the manuscripts, where I'm refused photos because it's the current exhibit. To think that all those stories were written and illustrated by hand. Gorgeous.

I miss a turn and end up at **Piazza della Santissima Annunciazziata**, where there's an enormous market of handicrafts, from woven yarns and silks to artesian cheese-making, original paintings to grains (toasted to taste like espresso), hat makers, jewelry and clothing designers, knitted sweaters, so much more. I fill another suitcase in my imagination. Then walk on towards **Sant Croce**, stopping for lunch at a little bistro with smells that entice. The piatta del giorno, my only meal of the day, is a lovely pasta with pumpkin and ground sausage, grilled chicken with green beans and roasted red & yellow peppers, a fine Valpolicella, caffé.

In a few blocks I'm finally at Sant Croce, with another huge market and the enormous Basilica. No discounts here, I have to pay the full E6 price. It's another mile plus back to my pallazo, after about eight already, but it's mostly along the river and eye-searing fun. On my arrival 'home' Olivia makes me a strong gin and tonic on the terrace, where I enjoy the setting sun and conversation with a couple from Brussels. I work til I can't, then sleep like a baby.

2 Novembre
It's quite a morning hike, but worth it as I walk then climb to the **Piazelle Michelangelo**,

http://mauiwriter.com/pm

with its spectacular views of Florence and the surrounding countryside. By the time I reach the Piazelle, I think I can't go any farther, but I'm so glad I do. The hilltop **Basilica of San Miniato al Monte**, with its lovely grounds, is run by only nine dedicated monks, one of whom calls me a taxi for the trip home. I feel sanctified, and the views are terrific!

Just past noon I am picked up for a 6-hour Wine Tour of the Chianti region with Massimo & Julio.

Take a Chianti wine tour:
http://mauiwriter.com/winetour

I meet new friends Megan and Francis, from San Francisco. It's serendipity.

Italy has twenty regions, of which Tuscany is one, with Florence (population 400k) the capitol of Tuscany, and south between Florence and Sienna lies Chianti (still part of the region of Tuscany). For a wine to be labeled Chianti, it must contain at least 80% of its Sangiovese grapes from the Chianti area, and the rest must also come from Tuscany (merlot, cabernet sauvignon, syrah).

We make three stops:

1. Sant Appiano, a tiny hill town just outside the Black Rooster area. Chianti Classico, other Tuscan wines, and evoo (extra virgin olive oil) are made here. French oak adds vanilla and berry notes. Large vats are Italian, for table wine, the everyday stuff.
- Rosé - definitely not a French one.
- Chianti DOCG - 90% sangiovese, 10% merlot, and way too young!
- Chianti Superiore - DOCG 100% sangiovese. nine months in French oak. It's not enough.

I didn't like any of these wines, but Julio poured me a nice grappa to get me down the road.

2. Panzanello - near Greve. Chianti Classico and Reserva from the famed Black Rooster area. In the 13th Century the Chianti League established this area, symbolized by a black rooster in a golden field. Luciano gave us a nice tour of this new winery, completed in 2009. They serve four wines: 2 black rooster classicos and 2 super tuscans. The winery also had three agro-tourisme apartments. They bottle 100k, 60k of which are Chianti Classico.

- Chianti Classico - 100% sangiovese grapes. super tuscan (better than the best at the last place)
- Chianti Classico Reserva - 18 months in French oak, 1 year in the bottle. 90% sangiovese grapes.
- Manuzio - 80% sangiovese/20% merlot, green harvested, hand-picked in July. Two years in oak. Two years in the bottle. Oh yes, now we're talking wine!
- Vindea - BEST. Wine of the goddess. Only 2500 bottles produced. 50% sangiovese, aged 3 years.

3. Greve - tiny village with a triangle square. I join Meg and Francis for tapas and a nice cappuccino. I'm speaking better French now than ever, asking Italians (in French) if they speak French or English, missing the cold caraffes of tap water, the little cookie with espresso, all things French.

As I bid aloha to Florence, flying off on Alitalia to London, I re-appreciate what a fabulous town Florence is and vow to practice my Italian for a future trip. Then I pick up my copy of Dan Brown's Inferno, left for me at my hotel, and re-live my Florence trip all the way home.

P.S. Did I mention my love affair with the
Arno River?
http://mauiwriter.com/arno

The excitement and gratitude, from that first day in Villefranche sur Mer until the last afternoon's sunfall in Florence, never left me. Each moment, was a future memory, dressed up as a jpeg. Each day - a blessing disguised as a blog entry. Everything was extraordinaire!

Home on the Road

For a week now I've wanted to process my French journey. But re-entry is tough, and being here now is critical - always, but especially during transitions.

> *"If it lights you, move that direction.*
> *If it drains your life force, move away.*
> *Trust your internal GPS. Your body knows."*

Leaving Florence, I spend two days in London with Peter and Stella and relatives. I get the big Greek welcome dinner with family and friends, then I'm shown all around this amazing city, sightseeing til we drop. The next day - a loving sendoff back to the states.

The first day or so back in Oregon, I love it. I'm landed, staying with family, running around getting my wheels and winter clothes together, enjoying the incredible colors of an Ashland autumn. A wine tasting with a good friend. Lunch with another. Then it descends like a dense fog, a funk, a post-trip depression. And friends start asking, "what's next?" as if I've already processed this latest journey or have any idea of my future.

I jump on Craigslist to sell my car, seek an island apartment rental. "Stay busy," I tell myself. "The time will pass quickly." I'm hit by a bug and go down for the week. It's cold, and in only days winter has come. At 6 am it's pitch black. Oh dear, I am not ready for this. I start wondering why I booked two weeks here, instead of flying straight on to Hawaii. Oh yes, I wanted time with Ashland friends, to enjoy this beautiful valley I have called 'home' for awhile. To remember.

Here's the rub. For those of us who travel, the rest of the world seems stuck. I have come home different. Friends are not. They seem too busy, too habitual, too stuck. We're speaking different languages. My friend Yvan says, *"the road is like a drug; it allows you to be time and space. You don't suffer hours as we feel when we stay in the same place."*

I'm still not done with the open road, the road less traveled, my adventure-lust. Coming back to my former home feels like an anticlimactic end to a life changing experience, and although I can't yet clearly articulate those changes, they are real. Friends call me a gypsy, a wanderer, a travel-junkie. More and more I am at home on the road, and returning is more difficult. Maybe I belong on the road.

"We travel not just to go, we travel to evolve. Embracing new experiences, endlessly changing horizons, and each brand new day as a way of living. We live for airports, planes, buses, boats, trains, road trips. We find clarity in the blur of the places zooming past us as we look through the window. This is our home. This will always be our home."   Stephanie Dandan

I think we need a people without borders movement. Having been a global citizen for at least thirty years, and meeting so many along the way who also find it tough to limit themselves to nationality, I find it more and more difficult to accept the arbitrary borders, set by wars, politicians, geography. The world over, people are all the same. We all want clean air, water, food, opportunity, to raise our families and care for our loved ones in peace and security, to be happy.

Every time I travel, I am reminded of this...and also of the borders imposed by corporate and political greed, the isolation and suffering created by these imposed borders. I still remember years ago seeing the iconic photo from space, showing our one precious planet earth, and thinking about that possibility. For awhile the United Nations gave me hope, but today the fight for territory is more ruthless than ever. Is there a way to live in the world, minimizing this effect? To transplant the best of cultures in our soil, to graft the best ideas in our backyards? To share this incredible blue planet?

I am missing Marché Forville, my morning café et pain chocolate, a train adventure to yet another little beach town or villàge perché. Mathieu. A day at a museum, soaking in the art of the French impressionists. As efficient as the French are, they haven't sacrificed beauty for efficiency. I miss the beauty...and the efficiency, the culture, the people-oriented benefits (great transportation, consumer protection, healthy food, better governance), long lunches. We can learn so much from the French.

What a glorious year! Still through all my travels, the very best part was meeting new friends...and seeing old ones. Beautiful souls all!

Take a look:
http://mauiwriter.com/friends

Let us be grateful to people who make us happy, they are the charming gardeners who make our souls blossom.
Marcel Proust

I end this year where I started it, back in the islands with family, to spend the winter near a warm beach, soaking it all in, consolidating, writing, editing, resting up for my next adventure. Making sense of my love-affair with France. And even though I really don't feel I'm 'home', and I already miss the French lifestyle, Maui has beautiful beaches...and I am always at home on a beach.

fin

We leave something of ourselves behind when we leave a place.
We stay there even though we go away.
And there are things in us we can find again only by going back there.
We travel to ourselves when we go to a place that we have covered a stretch of in our lives.

Night train to Lisbon

Meet the Author

Friends think of Karen as a travel guru. She thinks of herself as an adventure junkie. Whatever, she loves being on the road, tasting new experiences, art, cultures, food.

As a passionate entrepreneur, she created several businesses on the US mainland, in Hawaii, and the South Pacific, for many years brokering private islands and boutique resorts.

Today she's a journalist and published author who writes a regular newspaper column, freelances for many companies and publications, and is CEO of an editing and publishing company, specializing in photography books, memoir, cookbooks, fiction and non-fiction.

Traveling to over 90 islands and 60 countries, she has tales to tell. Stories from magical places pepper her writings, which are autobiographically inspired and informed.

"Life's a trip...so get out there
and enjoy this bright, beautiful planet."

Made in the USA
San Bernardino, CA
15 September 2017